CW00525981

Mind
for Hire

Mind for Hire

A practitioner's guide to management consulting

ROGER C. SMITH

University of Western Australia Press

First published in 2000 by
University of Western Australia Press
Nedlands, Western Australia 6907
www.uwapress.uwa.edu.au

Published with funding assistance from the Graduate School of Management, The
University of Western Australia.

National Library of Australia
Cataloguing-in-Publication entry:

Smith, Roger (Roger C.).
    Mind for hire: a practitioner's guide to management consulting.

    ISBN 1 876268 47 6 (pbk).

    1. Business consultants—Handbooks, manuals, etc. I. Title.

658.46

Produced by Benchmark Publications Management, Melbourne
Consultant editor Amanda Curtin, Curtin Communications, Perth
Designed by Ron Hampton, Pages in Action, Melbourne
Typeset in 10pt Sabon by Lasertype, Perth
Printed by Australian Print Group, Maryborough, Victoria

Foreword

Mind for Hire provides valuable insight into the business of management consulting and contributes significantly to the body of knowledge for management consultants in the Asia Pacific Region. It is clear from the points Professor Roger Smith raises, and from the content he has selected, that the breadth and depth of his understanding of the role of the management consultant is extensive. Professor Smith has lent this knowledge to those of us who are seeking not only clarification of the role of the management consultant, but a clearer understanding of the dynamics of the processes that are employed in this role.

Management consulting as a profession has developed considerably in the last twenty years. Today there is a different attitude towards management consulting. In the past, organizations employed consultants to assist them in bringing about changes only after identifying problems or impending failure. There is now a greater tendency to enlist external support as an ongoing policy, and consultants are often seen as the key players in bringing about changes that will ensure a more predictable outcome.

The title of this work is apt, because, as Professor Smith points out, it is the objective and unemotional position of the management consultant as a 'mind for hire'—an outsider looking in—that creates a distinct advantage when it comes to identifying problems and issues that are not always clear to those immersed in an organization.

Mind for Hire should prove a valuable tool for the newcomer to the industry, as well as providing some new and interesting dimensions for those management consultants looking for confirmation of existing processes and practices.

Richard J. W. Elliott, FIMC, CMC
First Vice-Chairman,
International Council of Management Consulting Institutes

I am very grateful to my editor, Amanda Curtin, and to University of Western Australia Press staff and consultants for their contribution in turning my original manuscript into a much more attractive and readable publication.

Contents

8. Learning to do the job **103**

Organizational and management skills 103
Interpersonal skills 104
Marketing and consulting technical skills 104
Self-learning 105
Mentoring 105
Education programs 105
On-the-job training 107

9. Running the business **111**

Business planning 112
The need for a business plan 112
Elements of a business plan 112
Types of business plan 113
Finance planning 114
Setting and assessing rates and fees 114
Overheads 116
Other charging methods 117
Budgeting 118
Administration 118
Marketing 119
Sources of new business 119
Elements of the marketing strategy 121

10. Learning from experience **123**

Hutton's research and consulting aphorisms 124
The problem is never about what it seems to be about 124
Completion will take three times as long as the last estimate 124
There is always a muddle in the middle 125
The most important item of equipment is the wastepaper basket 125
The right to practise is earned 125
Question the assumptions 126
Work where the problem is 127
Feelings are useful 127
Every structure tells a story 128
Other people's experiences are more useful than their solutions 129
Action begins where analysis begins 130

Tables, figures, abbreviations

List of tables

List of figures

List of abbreviations

AR	actual role
CEO	chief executive officer
CMC	Certified Management Consultant
EOI	expression of interest
IC	intellectual capital
ICMCI	International Council of Management Consulting Institutes
IMC	Institute of Management Consultants
MBA	Master of Business Administration
PD	Professional Development
PERT	program evaluation review technique
PR	prescribed role
RFP	request for proposal
RPO	role perceived by others
RPS	role perceived by self
TOC	Theory of Constraints
TOR	terms of reference
UBK	Unified Body of Knowledge

The organism in its totality is as essential to an explanation of its elements as its elements are to an explanation of the organism.

ARTHUR KOESTLER (1959)

A beginning

1

Management consulting has occupied a major part of my life for the past twenty years or so and has therefore had a great impact on me. Much of this experience has been gained in and around Perth, Western Australia, but a significant amount has been acquired in Canada, the United Kingdom, South East Asia and South Asia.

I came into consulting via earlier careers in school teaching, production chemistry, systems analysis, human resource management and university lecturing. While these career experiences stood me in reasonably good stead for consulting once I understood what it was all about, my early days in the profession largely involved trial and error, some obvious wins and losses, assignments where the outcome was vague to say the least, and generally an approach linked more to faith and hope than to competence and confidence.

While I have developed more competence and confidence over the years, the nature of the job is such that there are still a percentage of assignments I do that do not work well. I am still learning, and the ideas and approaches in this book are not those of an expert but those of a consultant who would like to share his knowledge and experience of the job and give a feel for its context, complexity and application.

Most of my work has been in the area loosely described as 'general consulting' rather than 'technical/specialist consulting', and has involved such assignments as organization analysis and design, project, process and performance improvement, institutional strengthening (a term common in international work with such agencies as the United Nations Development Program, the Australian Agency for International Development and the International Labour Organization) and strategic planning, as well as a number of research-oriented activities designed to assess the operation and results of various projects. In a sense, I do specialize in that I concentrate on performance improvement in order to achieve the client organization's goal.

In summary, I help to remove the performance constraints or obstacles that prevent goal achievement. I could perhaps be called a 'specialist generalist'.

The technical specialists tend to have an edge over the generalists in that technical areas such as computing, production and quality control, finance, safety and marketing are readily identifiable and accepted by managers as 'expert' areas where it is sensible to get assistance. Generalists are dealing with less tangible elements of organizational operation and have a harder task to justify and sell their services and also to evaluate the worth of their efforts. From recent discussions with users of consulting services, it appears that the trend is towards the increasing use of specialists. This, it seems to me, is edging consulting more towards contracting—an issue I return to in chapter 2.

While my background obviously colours my views on the topic, I believe that much of what I say applies to both types of consulting, and so I address both generalists and specialists in these pages.

THE ROLE OF CONSULTING IN ENTERPRISE

Consulting, in one form or another, has become an important part of professional activities. Some professions have come to include the word 'consulting' in their titles—for example, there are consulting architects, travel consultants, consulting engineers, taxation consultants. In a number of other professions, such as social work and general medical practice, consulting is an implied, though not specified, activity.

Many of the points I make, although aimed at consulting to management in organizations, will therefore have relevance to these other professions, particularly in regard to the nature of consulting, the establishment of relationships, and the generation and analysis of data. A common point, of course, is that we all work for, with and in organizations, but we are *not of them*—in the sense of being a part of them.

The consulting cycle described in chapter 6 is basically a problem-solving method that can profitably be used by anyone who has a problem to solve, including managers themselves.

GROWTH OF MANAGEMENT CONSULTING

Management consulting is the fastest growing area of consultancy in many countries, including Australia. The United Kingdom Business Statistics Office recently indicated that there had been a 200 per cent increase in the number of management consultants registered between 1985 and 1992. In Australia, the Institute of Management Consultants (IMC) has experienced a membership increase of 100 per cent over the past five years. Even so, the IMC has captured only around 10 per cent of the estimated 15,000 people who call themselves management consultants in Australia. The industry is reckoned to be worth $3.5 billion per annum in Australia and $50 billion worldwide.

Much of this growth has been caused by the liberalization, restructuring, downsizing, privatization or globalization of many organizations—big and small—in all sectors of economies, which has encouraged the expansion of the consulting profession to provide assistance to these organizations in solving the more complex problems that have arisen. Many of the people made redundant by such activities have become consultants to the organizations they have just left!

In addition to the growth in consulting practices, it is becoming increasingly common for organizations to appoint internal consultants in such areas as human resources management, health and safety, industrial relations and quality control. This is because the title 'consultant', and the associated required change in approach, are more in tune with the advisory nature of these staff positions, as opposed to their traditional 'tell and sell' directive method.

However, people working in these consultant positions often do not change their methods, because they are unfamiliar with the consultancy task as described in chapters 6 and 7.

Those who occupy managerial positions in organizations are becoming increasingly involved in the outsourcing of activities to consultants, which means that they have the responsibility of controlling and evaluating the consultant contribution—or lack of it—to their organizations. Learning about the consultant role and its place in assisting organizations will better equip them to exercise this responsibility.

There was a time when hiring a consultant was seen as an admission of failure. Now consultants are a part of the normal process of work. However, this does not mean that they are always accepted by those they work with or that they always contribute positively to organizational life.

ACCREDITATION OF CONSULTANTS

In the early 1990s, the IMC in Australia joined with the International Council of Management Consulting Institutes (ICMCI) to establish a Certified Management Consultant (CMC) qualification. This can only be granted to members of the institute upon completion of an examination, or recognition of prior experience, and retained by regular participation in professional development activities.

This move has been taken in view of the increasing professionalization of the discipline and the need by organizations to be able to readily identify consultants who are recognized and certified by a reputable and ethical institution.

The CMC is transportable between member countries and thus represents a universal accreditation of management consulting competence. More information about the CMC is available on the IMC's comprehensive web site designed for both clients and consultants.†

---

† Web site: www.management-consultants.com.au

Despite this, there is currently no requirement for would-be practitioners to get a licence to practise management consulting: anyone can hang up a shingle and tout for business. As noted above, it is estimated that there are more than 15,000 self-identified management consultants in Australia, of whom only some 1,200 are members of the professional representative body, the IMC. I believe there is thus a need to educate and train people who are anticipating a career in consulting.

Formal education and training in consulting methodology prevent newcomers from entering the field in the 'trial and error' mode, which is common to many people who label themselves consultants to organizations on the basis of technical skill and working experience—the way I described my entry. As new consultants soon find, there is a world of difference between applying expertise as an employee and applying it in an 'outsider' role. There are a number of books and articles that at least introduce the topic to those interested, and I hope that this book provides another that can be used in this way.

STRUCTURE OF THIS BOOK

Mind for Hire attempts to come to grips with the whole gamut of consulting—its nature, context and operational performance—and does so from my personal perspective, supported by information from many other people, who are acknowledged herein.

The 'nuts and bolts' of the profession, as I see it, are described in chapters 2 to 10. Chapter 11 allows me to present some final thoughts on the profession, and to include some controversial views that challenge the conventional wisdom, in order to provide a balance to the more traditional approach taken in the earlier chapters.

Appendix A gives readers an opportunity to apply theory, personal opinions and experience to a series of consulting situations that are typical of those faced by consultants and clients. Also included in this appendix is a longer case study that poses a number of issues common to small business and which presents an opportunity to use the consulting cycle, as described in chapter 6, which is a key feature of this book.

Appendix B provides a list of additional books and articles, including those from the *Journal of Management Consulting* (now *Consulting to Management*), which may be accessed to shed more light on the management consulting process.

I hope that for consultants, internal consultants and those who employ consultants, this book serves a useful purpose in making consulting interventions more acceptable, enjoyable and productive.

What does a management consultant do?

DEFINITIONS AND DESCRIPTIONS

The management consultant

In simple terms, a management consultant helps managers and their organizations to do things better and get better results. Would that this were a sufficient description!

That it is not sufficient is well illustrated by the questions and comments I get at social events when meeting new people, where one is usually asked, 'What do you do?'. My simple answer that I am a management consultant often leads to comments like:

'Oh, you're one of them, eh! Borrow their watch and tell them the time—ho, ho!'

'Does that mean you know better than them and can tell them what to do?'

'We had one of your lot in our business last year and it was no help at all. Didn't tell us anything we wanted to hear.'

'I hear you people charge up to $200 an hour. It must be a pretty good money-spinner.'

'Just how do you help people when you only consult and don't act!'

The IMC is more definitive in describing what management consultants do. It says that management consulting is an

7

independent and objective advisory service provided by qualified persons to clients in order to help them identify and analyse management problems or opportunities. Consultants, it says, may also be involved in recommending solutions or suggested actions with respect to these issues and may assist, when requested, in their implementation in order to help the client or client organization achieve its purposes and objectives.

A key distinction here is between a *management consultant*, who adopts a wide-ranging, management-focused and problem-solving approach to a client's needs, and a *specialist consultant*, concerned simply, for example, with advising on the purchase and installation of new information technology or on carrying out a training program. This distinction, however, is blurred, and many members of the IMC are specialist consultants.

In reality, the distinction is not binary but rather a continuum, with any one consultant occupying a particular position on that

---

The following tongue-in-cheek poem, written by 'Bernie Ramsbottom', was published in a 1981 issue of the Financial Times *in the United Kingdom and surfaced again in a recent article in the* Journal of Management Consulting. *No doubt Bernie would be taken to task today for presuming that all consultants are men!*

Of all the businesses, by far
Consultancy's the most bizarre.
For to the penetrating eye,
There's no apparent reason why,
With no more assets than a pen,
This group of personable men
Can sell to clients more than twice
The same ridiculous advice,
Or find, in such rich profusion,
Problems to fit their own solution.

continuum on a particular project or by preference in selling their service to a particular market.

As a further point of clarification, it should be noted that some trainers are also consultants and some professional speakers also consult, but merely being a trainer or a speaker does not automatically make one a consultant any more than being a consultant makes one a trainer or a speaker.

Two other descriptions I could suggest relating to the job of management consulting are:

- A consultant is someone who provides a specialized expertise, content, behaviour, skill or other resource to assist/help a client in improving the status quo. This intervention focuses on a specific client need.
- Consulting is aimed at some improvement in the future functioning of the client system—that is, positive change.

A consultant, then, is a *partner in change.*

Larry Greiner and Robert Metzger (1983) say that management consulting is an uncertain and evolving process conducted by a foreign intruder who muddles through by performing various problem-solving activities, while trying to maintain high professional standards and still attempting to meet the needs of the client.

In a particular 'Beetle Bailey' cartoon, the Sergeant says to Beetle that he sees him all over camp but never sees him do anything. Beetle, he claims, knows everyone and talks to everyone, but they do the work—so he queries: *What is your job title, anyway?* Beetle replies, *I'm a consultant.*

All this indicates that management consultants are on the outside looking in: that they examine problems and opportunities with a view to changing things for the better for people called clients, that they are qualified in some way, and that they advise, assist and help rather than execute or actually do. In other words, from a client perspective, the consultant is a 'mind for hire'. As I make clear throughout this book, however, no change can occur without the inside looking out—that is, change must be sanctioned and actioned by the organization members themselves.

The client

In the broadest sense of the term, the client is the organization engaging the consultant to provide help. However, from the consultant's point of view, the term 'client' often refers to the individual or individuals with whom he or she has the initial and/or ongoing contacts. Usually the client is a high-level manager (or sometimes a committee), but for assignments of limited scope, the client could be a lower level manager.

Consultants normally have contact with many other people during the course of an assignment, and I have found from experience that these other people need to be treated in much the same way as the contracting client is treated in relation to responsibilities, techniques and ethics. However, the brief or proposal must spell out to whom the consultant will be primarily responsible for his or her performance.

The client–consultant relationship

There is no doubt that it is difficult to get a job, or to carry it out successfully, without having a reasonably good relationship with the client—and that relationship is as much about how the client perceives the consultant as a person as it is about the consultant's consulting skills.

The main difference between the manager (the client) and the consultant is that the consultant is outside the organization and the manager is inside it. This means that the consultant has no authority while the manager does, and the manager has to live with the results of the intervention while the consultant can walk away to intervene in another organization. The similarities are that both are qualified (in their own ways) and both examine things with a view to change and improvement.

A client should not use a consultant because he/she has more knowledge or better analytical skills or fancier presentation skills. Consultants should be used because they know less, not more, than their clients. They have value because they are not attached to the rooted assumptions—the 'inertia'—of the organization (Goldratt 1990).

It is the nexus between the consultant and the client in regard to examining things and changing them that forms the main basis for the operation and outcome of a consultancy. The client uses the consultant for leverage purposes—that is, to add external knowledge and skill to the internal knowledge, skill and understanding of the operational context.

Consulting, then, is certainly not synonymous with implementing, delivering, instructing or executing, although it may include any of these activities when done in conjunction with the client—the decision-maker for these activities.

The nature of the client–consultant relationship is discussed in detail in chapter 5.

The way the consultant works

I believe that it is the way I work that makes me a consultant—that is, the particular process that I use in order to fit the various definitions given above. One of the more useful descriptions of consulting comes from Geoffrey Hutton (1979, p. 2): 'consulting is the process of helping other people to solve problems they are having problems solving'. In this sense, it has many similarities with counselling, a function that prevails in psychotherapy, psychiatry, psychology and social work.

Hutton is a follower of the Tavistock Institute (United Kingdom) collaborative approach to understanding enterprise problems, the solutions to which inevitably involve individual and social change. The 'Tavvy' uses a field theory approach that regards behaviour as being determined by a field of interrelated forces. Thus field theory holds that a particular event may best be understood as the outcome of other interacting events in the larger field in which it occurs. It is therefore unlikely that notions of simple cause and effect will explain social behaviour, either inside or outside organizations.

The task of the consultant is seen as that of discovering the existence and nature of these different forces and showing their relationships in facilitating or inhibiting social development.

As Elliott Jaques (1951) describes in his classic book on the Glacier Metal Company project, in this context a professional relationship between a consultant and a client implies shared responsibility for what happens as a result of the joint analysis of the problem that brought them together.

CONCEPTS

The nature of organizations

I am also a follower of the Tavistock school of thought and an admirer of the work of such people as Eric Trist, Fred Emery, Jaques, Cyril Sofer, Lisl Klein and Harold Bridger, even though they practised many years ago and do not have the high profile of American experts such as Fred Luthans, Peter Drucker, Douglas McGregor, Tom Peters and Kenneth Blanchard.

The Glacier Metal Company project, noted above, was an innovative example of how unconscious forces in group behaviour and the unwitting collusion between groups, for purposes of which they are only dimly aware, are vital factors in the process of social adaptation. In most groups, there is a deep anxiety and suspicion that insight into one's own group behaviour will lead to the release of destructive forces and cause irreparable damage to the group.

There would not be many management consultants who have not had their efforts at investigating the reasons for poor group performance thwarted by this felt, but often not recognized, anxiety and suspicion.

It is primarily out of the work of the Tavistock Institute that the so-called 'socio-technical systems' approach to organization analysis/diagnosis and development was born. The operation of an organization is the result of a complex interaction between the social system and the technical system, and this interaction is subject to considerable movement and subtle change, despite the more or less consistent cultural heritage that develops over time. Given this approach and its implications, it would be a naive consultant or manager who believed that a concentration on one aspect of the organization's operation will improve performance.

Social science, psychology and psycho-social analysis play a role in management, and in consultancy, that is equally as important as that played by mathematics, science, computing, statistics, accounting and finance. Associated with this quantitative–qualitative dichotomy is the concept of the official system versus the unofficial system explained in one of my earlier books (Smith 1994).

A chapter entitled 'It pays to understand the underworld' highlights the importance of knowing how the official and unofficial systems work together to result in performance. Consultants who do not come to grips with both systems will, sadly, be often led astray in any attempt to analyse and understand organizational operation.

However, consultants should be aware that complete knowledge and understanding of an organization is unattainable, because complete analysis and the construction of reality maps are impossible—if only because of the dynamic nature of organizations.

Consulting versus contracting

Consulting should not be confused with contracting, which is more akin to hiring a person or persons to work on a routine organizational managerial task as a de facto employee for a specified period. (Such people are now being called 'interim managers' in the United Kingdom literature, and there is a recently established journal called the *Journal of Interim Management and Consultancy*.)

This is a key point to understand, because many organizations, particularly those in the public sector, hire people under contract (often, as noted earlier, people they have just made redundant) for set periods on organizational tasks and call them 'consultants'. In most instances, this is a misnomer and a further illustration of the difficulty that exists in defining the role of a consultant.

Consulting as a socio-psychological process

Timothy Clark (1995) considers that it is useful to look at consulting through a new lens—that is, as the art of impression management—because in the face of strong competition and a weak client knowledge base about consulting, consultants must persuade clients that their service is worth buying.

He also uses the dramaturgical metaphor to describe consulting, saying that the principles of theatre — actions, setting, scripts, etc. — undergird the way in which consultants seek to manage their relationships with clients and come to comprehend this. In this sense, he sees consulting as very much a socio-psychological process.

My experience leads me to agree with this approach. Certainly, there is a lot of competition in the consulting profession. Clients often choose a consultant on the basis of personality preference, and the consultancy action may take the form of a drama, with plots, counterplots, actors with different agendas, and unexpected twists and turns complicating the process.

THE NATURE OF CONSULTING

Characteristics

Management consulting is a service and therefore shares many of the characteristics of other types of service. It is these characteristics, plus the definitional controversies that surround the word 'consultant', that make the provision of consulting services such a demanding and complex task.

The characteristics of consulting are discussed as follows.

Consulting is intangible

There is nothing to be seen, heard, felt, tasted or smelled in the provision of consulting service, and clients often do not know what they want to get until they get what they do not want! The brief sets out the expectations, which, of course, may or may not be met.

Consulting involves direct interaction between buyer and seller and the two are inseparable

In order for the delivery of a service to be complete, the consultant and client have to interact directly. Service is a relational activity based upon social intercourse between the two parties. The relationship can be:

- task interactive (concentrating on solving a client's already identified problem); or
- people interactive (where the client is unaware or imprecise about what will best serve the organization's interest and how to go about remedying a situation).

The first is called, in consulting jargon, a *purchase model* and the second is a *doctor–patient model*.

Edgar Schein (1969) has suggested a *process (or process consulting) model* that is somewhere between these two extremes and aims at making consulting a method of helping clients to help themselves and is thus more concerned with process and people than with task.

Consulting involves heterogeneity

This refers to the extent to which consulting can be standardized. While elements of the specialist role could be said to be homogeneous, heterogeneity tends to be the norm with general consulting, because every new working context is different. From the client point of view, however, homogeneity is expected at least in relation to consistent quality—that is, a high-quality service level is required each time a consultancy is assigned. For the consultant, this means 'selling' service by performing well, because the client is being asked to buy a promise.

Consulting is perishable

Consulting services are perishable, since they are destroyed in the process of consumption and cannot be stored. Although a result such as a report is less perishable, if it is not acted upon it may as well be destroyed.

Implications of these characteristics

There are, of course, many implications that flow from these characteristics. These include the following:

- Quality is hard to determine.

- The outcome is dependent on the quality of interaction with clients.
- The interaction experience can influence perceptions of the outcome, whatever its quality.
- A client can't purchase exactly the same consulting service twice.
- Consulting services are sold, and then produced and consumed simultaneously.
- Consulting is, of necessity, concerned with the management of impressions, as described by Clark (1995).

Thomas Greenbaum (1990) suggests that the typical objections to consultants arise out of the nature of consulting, as described above. His 'objections' list includes:

- You are selling an intangible.
- You are selling without a guarantee.
- You are often selling to a poorly defined need.
- Clients feel threatened by consultants—by their expertise, by their cost and by their threat to control and security.
- Many people feel that only experts in their particular business can help or that they are experts and do not need consultants.

Consultants find that, in organizations, there are many 'no' people and few 'yes' people.

OPERATIONS

I have found that much of what I do as a consultant is similar to what I did as a researcher producing theses and academic articles as a part of my academic career. There is a relationship between consulting and research in that many of the elements are the same (gathering data, analysis, synthesis), though their application and the objectives differ. Tables 1 and 2—from Peter Block (1981), and my own experience—illustrate the differences.

My own encounters with clients seem to be mainly of two types: sharing information and advice in consultations within a short time-frame, and contracting for longer term projects or studies.

Table 1   Research versus consulting—characteristics

Factor	Research	Consulting
Problem	Defined by researcher, more open-ended	Defined by client, often with consultant
Time-scale	Longer term, relatively open-ended	Shorter term, more rigid
Objective	New knowledge and new theories—understanding	Improved organization performance—action
Ownership of information	Usually publicly available	Generally confidential
Academic rigour	Methodologically tight, theoretical	Minimum level appropriate, pragmatic
Evaluation	External—by peers	Internal—by client

Table 2   Research versus consulting—approach

Research approach	Consulting approach
Interested in all factors that affect problem at hand	Interested in factors that are under the control of client and affect problem
Comprehensive and complete diagnosis essential	Complete and comprehensive diagnosis unnecessary; it can overwhelm and prevent action
Can be done alone. The organization does not have to be involved as part of research team	Client's involvement at every step of process is necessary and important
Tries to eliminate bias and intuition of researcher. Heavy emphasis on objectivity and hard data	Consultants are paid for their own bias and intuition—it is called judgment. All of the consultant's feelings and perceptions are used as 'hard' data
Essentially neutral towards whether the organization approves of study outcomes	Deeply concerned about the attitude of the client to consultancy outcome

Both these encounters involve the use of what I call the *consulting cycle*, but the longer term contracts or studies also involve another critical activity: *project management.*

The consulting cycle (see chapter 6) used in both types of encounter is, essentially, an analysis/synthesis/solution generation methodology, while project management (see chapter 7) involves a large component of managerial/administrative tasks.

ROLES

There are various roles that can be undertaken by, or sometimes forced upon, the consultant in performing a consulting contract.

Role analysis

A role consists of the total pattern of expected behaviour, interactions and sentiments for an individual holding a job. A role analysis and subsequent role description for a job tells us more about a job and what is expected of the job holder than the relatively formal and sterile job description. Thus the job analyst's task could well be supplemented by the work of a person I call a 'role analyst'.

When considering roles, it is useful to understand the 'role analyst' basic framework, which suggests that there are four different perceptions of role:

- the prescribed role (PR)—for example, the job description;
- the actual role (AR)—the job as it is actually performed;
- the role perceived by self (RPS)—how the incumbent sees himself or herself in terms of status, value, expertise, etc.;
- the role perceived by others (RPO)—how others see the job and its performance, outputs, status, value, expertise, requirements, etc.

It is important that the consultant's RPS coincides more or less with the RPO (where the client is O). Different perceptions and expectations have caused the downfall of many a consulting contract.

Models

I look at consulting roles in a way similar to that in which management researchers consider the various roles of the manager as described by Henry Mintzberg (1973)—leader, decision-maker, liaison, information disseminator, conflict resolver, resources allocator and so on.

Consulting, like managing, can involve a variety of roles, depending on circumstances, preference or pressure. There are many ways in which these roles have been described, three of which have already been mentioned: the purchase model or role, the doctor–patient model or role, and Schein's (1969) process model or role.

Others that come to mind are professional adviser and counsellor, role consultant, qualified resource (industry or specialist content knowledge/skill, such as travel, mining, agriculture, computers) and change agent.

Decision-maker, salesperson of proprietary products, and packager of standard services are roles that can be exercised but which can cause problems, because they imply authority and a 'whatever your problem, I have the answer' approach. The promoters of standard packages and packaged solutions suffer, it seems to me, from the 'if your only tool is a hammer, everything looks like a nail' syndrome.

Another set of roles is suggested by Fritz Steele (1975):

- *Teacher:* using didactic processes to train clients (students);
- *Student:* receiving instruction from clients or learning about behaviour in organizations as a result of consulting. In many respects, this learning experience lies at the core of becoming a good consultant. The role is rich in the number and variety of experiences available that can expand a consultant's knowledge and skill;
- *Detective:* trying to discover evidence and fit it together to help the consultant and client develop accurate pictures of the system, its problems and its strengths;
- *Barbarian:* a violator of comfortable but limiting norms, able to behave less politely than members of the organization and raise 'dangerous' issues and ask 'taboo' questions;

- *Clock:* a timer or clock for clients, as regular visits remind them that it is time for them to do something so that they have something to show to the consultant;
- *Monitor:* related to the clock role but more specific in terms of observing and commenting on project/client progress;
- *Talisman:* presence provides a sense of legitimacy and security that allows the client to experiment in areas into which he or she would not normally venture;
- *Advocate:* for the values and principles of relations between the organization and the individual—decent, non-exploitative, productive, honest, trustworthy. If they are at odds with the client values, the consultant should retire or could be fired;
- *Ritual pig:* serving as an outside threat that needs to be 'killed off' (fired, resisted, challenged) in order for the system to develop enough sense of solidarity and potency to be able to begin some difficult self-change. People often resort to this type of denial and projection in order to transfer their stress or problem to an 'outsider' so that they can preserve an image of strength, security and harmony.

This has been my favourite framework of metaphors for many years—probably because I have occupied these roles a number of times, even if I did not always realize it at the time. The one role I do always recognize when I am in it is that of ritual pig—it is pretty hard to miss.

No matter what reason a client might have for hiring a consultant, the consultant generally does not know as much about the client's organization as the client does; therefore, the client must expect that any solutions implemented will require active client participation.

What the consultant offers

Consultants are usually more expensive per day than the average manager, so what criteria can they use to sell their services? One cannot be a consultant unless one is consulted, and the key to getting clients who want consultation is marketing. Thus the selling or marketing of one's services is a vital factor in surviving as a consultant—and I have found that a large part of my service is myself.

The vital components in providing a service as a consultant are similar to those necessary for any service provider—personal involvement with key client personnel, availability to clients and responsiveness to the needs of the client organization.

The strengths of management consultants, as defined by the IMC, are that they:

- provide an independent and external viewpoint;
- have special qualifications/skills including exposure to many different organizations and industries—they have been around and seen a lot and not much surprises them;
- offer a temporary professional service without the overheads and regulation associated with employment;
- can help justify decisions already made;
- can help resolve sensitive, confidential problems or issues that are difficult for insiders to face.

THE PROS AND CONS OF CONSULTING

I am often asked why I became a consultant and continue to practise. The profession has pros and cons. The pros include independence, challenge, variety, and opportunities to work in different contexts and tackle different problems. The cons include irregular living conditions/travel, financial risk, uncertain cash flows, and the pressures and stress of trying to improve organizational performance without the authority to decide on methods and implement them.

For the self-employed consultant or the consultant who is part of a small partnership or company, the financial rewards are not outstanding. In a survey conducted by the Western Australian Chapter of the IMC, 80 per cent of consultants fell into this category (that is, outside the big national and international consultancies) and their average individual gross earnings were *declared* as being around $80,000 per annum. This is about two and a half times the Australian average annual earnings and on about the same level as a university associate professor—who may be also operating as a consultant and thus earning considerably more.

For anyone contemplating becoming a self-employed consultant or a partner in a small consulting business, the pros noted above and the possible financial returns need to be weighed against the cons described and the benefits of the security of employment.

What's needed to do the job?

FUNCTIONAL VERSUS CONSULTING SKILLS

A look at the range of areas in which consulting takes place gives some indication of the diverse functional theoretical bases upon which it depends. These areas include:

- general and strategic management;
- financial management;
- marketing and distribution management;
- production management;
- human resources management;
- information technology/knowledge management;
- small business management;
- public sector management;
- productivity and performance improvement.

The nature of management consulting requires that its practitioners be familiar with one or more of these functional areas/subjects. People usually do not go into management consulting without some level of disciplinary expertise.

For example, my main discipline was human resources management and associated aspects of organization analysis, diagnosis and design. My first consulting job was in a dry cleaning establishment in Saskatoon, Canada, and involved an investigation of the structure, jobs and people in relation to the business objectives and the processes used to achieve these. I carried it out as a research assignment rather than a consulting assignment, and thus my intervention did not lead to any changes. After a few more contracts where the process and outcome were less than satisfactory, it dawned on me that functional skill and knowledge were not enough. Consultancy itself involves a body of knowledge and a set of techniques unique to carrying it out, and makes sense only when change occurs in the client system.

Functional expertise is usually the primary reason for people entering the profession—they have a skill resource and feel it is saleable in the market. In the same way, functional expertise is often the basis of selection for moving a person into a management position in an organization, but such expertise alone will not be sufficient for that person to achieve success in the managerial role. The skills of management must also be acquired.

For consultants, the acquisition of consulting skills is as important to them as is the acquisition of management skills to managers.

CONSULTING AS A PROFESSION

Associated with the above points is the claim that management consulting is a profession. A profession is a calling or vocation in which members, possessing certain attributes, provide beneficial services to clients under strictly specified conditions.

My IMC colleagues and I consider that we belong to a professional group because we satisfy the characteristics of a profession, as follows:

- We possess a variety of skills and qualities, the acquisition of which requires extensive education, training and/or experience.
- We provide services that are based on technical and process proficiency, which in turn is recorded in an appropriate *body of knowledge.*
- We abide by a code of ethics and practise standards in the delivery of services to clients and in relationships with competitors and with the public.

- We establish fees that are fixed with respect to the amount and type of work to be performed and are not contingent on an outcome of some event (as is sometimes the case in other professions, such as law).

The Unified Body of Knowledge (UBK), which is the IMC's document describing the profession, its application and responsibilities, names three levels of consultant:

- management consultants, who operate in this job area but are self-identified and not members of the institute;
- professional management consultants, who operate in this job area and are members of the institute;
- CMCs, who operate in this job area, are members of the institute and have completed the institute requirements for certification.

The UBK is a good guide to the things that consultants should know. In summary, the knowledge framework includes:

1. management consulting as a process and a profession;
2. general knowledge about the nature and environment of business, basic business law and economics, the managerial process and the attributes of government and non-profit institutions;
3. general or entity management—including top management and organizing principles;
4. functional areas within enterprises—finance and accounting, logistics, marketing, human resources, research and development, public relations, information systems;
5. technical disciplines—mathematics and statistics, quantitative and management science techniques, information technology, communication techniques.

Any one consultant is unlikely to have all the above, but at a minimum would need expert knowledge of 1 and one or more of 4 and 5, and basic knowledge of 2 and 3.

In the United Kingdom, the IMC has adopted a credit accumulation and transfer framework that is used to grant CMC admission by competency assessment. The framework includes four different types of competence that need to be demonstrated:

- management consulting competence;
- management competence;
- relevant specialist technical competence (for example, finance, information technology, human resources management);
- PESTLE (political, economic, social, technological, legal and environment) competence and ACT (acting, communicating and thinking) competence.

SUMMARY OF REQUIRED CONSULTING SKILLS

Extracting the essence of what the UBK and the IMC in the United Kingdom are saying, as well as looking at my own experience, results in the following interpretation of the attributes and skills that a consultant should have in order to practise effectively. Of these, the ones least likely to have been acquired by a new consultant are marketing skills and consulting technical skills.

Functional skills

Skills are required in one or more business areas in which the consultant has a formal qualification and/or experience—for example, human resources management, systems analysis, process engineering.

Organizational and management skills

The consultant must have an ability to access (or have accessed) the various theories that have been developed in relation to organizations and their management, and to apply them in the knowledge of their strengths and weaknesses. This ability is noted in points 2 and 3 of the UBK framework.

It would be difficult to be an effective management consultant without having had some exposure to the basics of organizational structure and design, decision-making, planning and control, motivation, communication, unofficial work systems, conflict and change, organizational culture, leadership, management and administrative roles and practice, individual and group behaviour, team building, learning, and so on.

Consulting technical skills

The ability to apply the key techniques of consulting cycle skills (see chapter 6) and project management skills (see chapter 7) is essential.

Consulting cycle skills

These encompass the approach used by a management consultant to help clients: determining the cause of problems, constraints or inefficiencies; identifying alternative solutions; selecting the most desirable alternative; and implementing the chosen solution using either quantitative or qualitative tools/methods, or both, as appropriate.

Project management skills

These include proposal writing; planning, controlling and documenting assignments; and presenting results to clients.

Interpersonal skills

Interpersonal skills are personal qualities that make an individual amiable to others and effective in accomplishing desirable objectives through others. They can be *inherent* attributes such as intelligence, health/appropriate appearance and energy and empathy, all of which are desirable at a high level. They can also be *developed* attributes such as an understanding of people and their behaviour, authenticity, integrity (fairness, honesty, ethics, dependability), courage, objectivity, ambition, problem-solving ability, judgment, communications ability, psychological maturity (ability to cope with frustration, ambivalence, and uncertainty—in other words, the ability to cope with life). These developed attributes are the foundation of the *process consulting skill* described by Edgar Schein (1969).

Marketing skills

Every consultant requires, to some extent, expertise in marketing, because the acquisition of clients is the key to survival. Marketing skill needs to be developed through course work, reading or talking to experienced consultants, so that the approach is taken in a systematic and cost-effective way. Approaches to marketing are discussed in chapter 9—but it is a truism that consultants are generally happier doing a job than marketing their services.

A PROCESS APPROACH TO CONSULTING

In regard to the process consulting skill noted above, Fritz Steele (1975) considers that whether one is a generalist or a technical specialist, the behavioural science consultation model seems to be universal in application. This is because even the technical 'expert' must understand the nature of change, the change process and the elements of individual and group behaviour. The best advice in the world will not be used by a client if he or she rejects it for defensive reasons or if the client system is not organized properly to put it into practice.

Thus, he claims, the basis of all consulting should be process consulting because of its fundamental tenet of being a helping, cooperative process and because it supports the primacy of learning to the consulting role.

CONFLICTS FACED BY THE CONSULTANT

Steele suggests that consultants have to deal with conflicting forces ('existential dilemmas', as he calls them) that both help and block learning at the same time. These conflicting forces are often not easily recognized, even by experienced consultants, and so they are worth summarizing to bring them into focus in this discussion of what's needed to do the job.

Each consultant has to find his or her own way to resolve dilemmas so that learning is increased and blockages are reduced or eliminated.

Performance versus learning

If you strive always to perform tasks to the highest level of performance of which you are capable, you will tend to choose to do those things that you can do well already (the hammer and nail syndrome again—if the only tool you have is a hammer, all you see is nails). Over time, this will result in relatively little learning of new skills.

If you want always to appear smooth and competent and ready with the answers, rather than unsure and willing to try something new, recognize that you will probably get stuck where you are in terms of skill.

Being a learner is harder than being an expert.

In reality, it is best to balance roles so that clients recognize that you have expertise without being an 'expert', and that you are willing to learn along with the client, given that neither of you begins from ground zero. It is also advisable to choose projects now and again that take you out of your comfort zone.

Paradoxically, this can require a fair degree of *unlearning*, because the dynamics of organizational life mean that the solutions of the past are unlikely to be applicable to present problems.

Open and closed systems

If you have no model or system at all for analysing behaviour, you are unlikely to make much use of your immediate experience or learn much from it. Conversely, if you have a single, tightly organized, closed system for thinking about organizational behaviour, you are also unlikely to learn much, since you throw away or distort data that do not fit your system.

You need enough of a closed system model to be able to organize perceptions, but it needs to be open and flexible enough to let new patterns come into focus.

In consulting work, an open system model enables you to concentrate on what is happening and then make inferences later. A closed system model tends to make you jump to immediate inferences from what is happening, which can fog observation.

Action and processing

If true learning is to occur, you need both to have experiences (action) and to use those experiences (processing) to make generalizations that can be incorporated in your own repertoire of skills and attitudes. That is, having experiences is a necessary, but not sufficient, condition for learning.

The more you jump from action to action without getting client feedback, or making notes to help sort out what happened, or listening to tapes (if made), or communicating experiences to others or observing reactions, the less chance that you will learn much that is new from your actions.

It is easy to become obsessed with doing rather than processing (thinking): action can be seen and looks like accomplishment, while processing is less visible and less results-oriented.

Action and processing should occur as closely together as possible for best results.

Stimulation threshold and overload

On the one hand, you need a high enough level of stimulation, challenge and newness in a situation to reach your personal threshold of sensitivity, but, on the other hand, you don't want that situation being so stimulating, demanding or threatening that it leads to your main concern being survival.

Seek consultancies that are challenging and somewhat beyond your present facility, but not too far beyond. Anxiety and fear usually result in a retreat into old behaviours that are not relevant to dealing with challenge in new situations.

Internal and external standards of growth

Is it better to use internal or external standards to determine your learning as a consultant or your success as a consultant?

The external standards are not well set, despite the generation of a number of requisite skills and attitudes for consultants (see chapter 8 for these qualitative requirements). This can result in uncertainty and anxiety when you use comparison with others as a measure. The great difference in areas of knowledge and skills required also makes such comparison hard.

The only answer is to develop your own internal standards to determine whether you are learning, growing and practising in the direction and at the rate relevant to your own time and needs. Run your own race!

COMMUNICATION

As in many other professions, communication is the vital thread that holds the processes of management consulting together. It is a key component of interpersonal skill.

The traditional interpersonal communication model considers one person as sender and one (or more) as receiver/s. I see that all people involved in communication are both senders and receivers during the same transaction (although the initiator is probably responsible for managing the transaction), and feedback in both directions is the critical factor in its success. It is essentially a process of influence, with the objective being understanding, acceptance and action.

Communication can be oral or written, and both forms involve the elements in these models in varying degrees and importance. In both, also, the implied or meta message (body language, writing style, timing, location, etc.) can be as significant as the overt or expressed message.

In the management consulting environment, barriers to communication can be many and include:

- know-it-all attitude;
- inability to understand technical language;
- inadequate background or knowledge;
- poor organization of ideas;
- differences in perception;
- prejudice or bias;

- personality conflicts;
- tendency not to listen;
- resistance to change;
- lack of credibility;
- inability to understand non-verbal communication;
- hostile attitude;
- lack of feedback;
- inappropriate physical appearance;
- differences in status or position;
- information overload;
- lack of trust;
- fear of distortion or omission of information;
- too many gatekeepers;
- poor timing of the message;
- defensiveness.

These barriers can apply to the consultant or the client or both. A look at this long list makes one wonder how we ever make contact at the understanding level at all! Obviously, we do on many occasions, but it usually does not happen automatically or without a great deal of time and effort, particularly when dealing with the larger operational and conceptual issues.

ETHICS

The subject of ethics is one that must be considered at some stage by a new consultant. Adherence to ethical standards is a benefit to both consultants and clients. Each consultant has a responsibility to him/herself, and to the profession, to work to these standards and to encourage others to do the same.

The IMC Code of Professional Conduct, spelled out in the UBK, has been developed to assist consultants deal with ethical issues. All members agree to abide by the code, as follows:

- *Confidentiality:* A member will treat client information as confidential and will neither take personal advantage of privileged information gathered during an assignment nor enable others to do so.

- *Unrealistic expectations:* A member will refrain from encouraging unrealistic expectations or promising clients that benefits are certain from specific management consulting services.
- *Commission/financial interests:* A member will not accept commissions, or remuneration or other benefits from a third party in connection with recommendations to a client without the client's knowledge and consent, nor fail to disclose any financial interest in goods or services that form part of such recommendations.
- *Assignments:* A member will accept only assignments that the member has the skills and knowledge to perform.
- *Conflicting assignments:* A member will avoid acting simultaneously in potentially conflicting situations without informing all parties in advance that this is intended.
- *Conferring with clients:* A member will ensure that before accepting any engagement, a mutual understanding of the objectives, scope, work plan and fee arrangement has been established and that any personal, financial or other interests that might influence the conduct of the work have been disclosed.
- *Recruiting:* A member will refrain from inviting an employee of a client to consider alternative employment without prior discussion with the client.
- *Approach:* A member will maintain a fully professional approach in all dealings with clients, the general public and fellow members.
- *Other management consultants:* A member will ensure that other management consultants carrying out work on behalf of the member are conversant with and abide by the Code of Professional Conduct.

In addition to the code, there are a number of 'discreditable acts' and 'discreditable behaviours' listed in the IMC by-laws. For example, work done on the basis of payment on results is considered a discreditable act, and entering into any arrangement that directly or indirectly reflects on the objectivity and impartiality of the advice given to clients is considered a discreditable behaviour.

While the code represents a comprehensive list and covers the main issues likely to be faced by a consultant, it is likely that other issues could arise that are not included. In these cases, it is left to the integrity and personal moral values of the consultant (and the client, if appropriate) for resolution.

In one instance early in my career, the client had a hidden agenda, which was to make use of my manager interview summaries as a means of sorting out his management team and reducing it in numbers. Although we had what I thought was a clear set of objectives in relation to determining procedural and operational issues, it was not so. If this agenda had been a stated objective in the brief, I would have had no part of it, but as events unfolded I was an unwitting partner in acting against my personal ethics.

The issue of ethics is a minefield that eventually becomes a matter for personal decision-making.

DO YOU HAVE WHAT IT TAKES?

For anyone contemplating taking up a consulting role, my question would be: 'Do you have what it takes to be a consultant?'.

Besides the normal requirements desired of people who take up organizational positions of responsibility — such as self-motivation, ability to make decisions, and skill in one or more functional areas — there are certain requirements that are specific to the consulting role.

I see them as a willingness to work long hours, the ability to be a good listener, objectivity, a high level of tolerance, the ability to dig for information, the intestinal fortitude to tell the truth as you see it, and a capacity to bear criticism and not take it to heart.

Judgment, which has already been mentioned, is an important skill for consultants. It has been described as deciding what to do when you don't (or can't) know what to do, but you sense that you have to do something fast. But how do you learn to be a good judge? Probably only through the experience of making many decisions and living with, and learning from, the consequences.

While it is useful to know what is needed to do the job, it is just as important to know how to acquire the skills, attitudes and knowledge involved, and this is the focus of chapter 8.

The management consultant's working context

THE INDIVIDUAL CONSULTANT

As a consultant, my primary workplace is the client's premises, even though I have an office in which to sit and think, plan, write proposals, write working papers, analyse data, write reports, and attend to the administrative detail of running a consultancy.

My work stands or falls mainly on what takes place or does not take place at the client site or sites. It is there that contacts are made, data are gathered, findings are shared and discussed, and agreed solutions are implemented.

My clients have included privately owned business firms, both large and small; government agencies and organizations; not-for-profit non-government organizations such as universities and hospitals; professional enterprises such as engineering, medical and accounting firms; and other areas such as unions and sports associations.

I have operated at the general management level and at all other levels in these enterprises.

THE WIDER SCENE

The range of consultants working in management consulting is as diverse as the market they serve—from the big firms like the PA Consulting Group, Ernst & Young, and PriceWaterhouseCoopers, to small businesses and single operators, and from generalists to specialists. Also, of course, many academics add consulting services to their regular job.

Consulting, which began in its current form in 1914, when Edwin Booz established Business Research Services in Chicago, is big business. Andersen Consulting is the world leader, with 1998 revenue of US$7.5 billion and just over 63,000 consultants at that time. Some other 'big players' in the profession are McKinsey & Co., KPMG Consulting, Deloitte Touche Tohmatsu, Boston Consulting Group, and Booz, Allen & Hamilton.

As well as working alone, I have often worked as part of a multidisciplinary team. It is becoming increasingly common for small consulting businesses and sole operators to form alliances in bidding for work, in order to be more competitive with the big players.

THE SCENE IN WESTERN AUSTRALIA

The conclusions arising from a benchmark study carried out by the Western Australian Chapter of the IMC (Jarosch 1997) give a good feel for the context of consulting in Western Australia, and anecdotal evidence suggests that surveys in other States would elicit similar results.

It should be noted, however, that non-respondents to this study included some large practices and some successful smaller practices, and so the results need to be seen in this context. The charge-out rates and billing income figures, in particular, are relevant only to those who responded.

The conclusions reached, on the basis of the survey data as analysed, were as follows:

A consultant in Western Australia would most likely have the following 'standardised' profile.

- runs a sole operator practice, which is relatively new (less than 5 years old) and which is unlikely to grow larger for lifestyle and economic reasons;

- has a variable chargeable hourly rate of [up to] $250, with an average rate of approximately $128 per hour (dependent on the assignment), and works full time, approximately [40] hours per week, as a consultant, taking approximately 3 weeks' scheduled block annual leave as well as shorter 'opportunity' leave periods;
- has a basic undergraduate qualification;
- has public liability insurance but not professional indemnity insurance unless required by a client;
- works from home or an office located in the Perth metropolitan area;
- serves mainly larger private sector clients such as the mining industry;
- acquires work by invitation with little or no competition;
- focuses primarily on business improvement services and is working on from one to several assignments simultaneously;
- allocates only minimal resources to marketing their services and depends heavily on personal contacts for work;
- takes in a gross [income] of approximately [$80,000+] which after costs would leave a profit of [about $50,000+ per annum];
- is the primary equity owner in the business;
- uses the accounting package MYOB;
- has various financial and quality performance criteria.

There is a need for more research to be undertaken into the various acceptable quantitative and qualitative performance criteria for financial and quality assessment, so that some guidelines can be developed for the consulting industry.

There is a need and place for initiatives to be taken by consulting groups and consulting associations to further develop practice management improvement.

There was evidence from this survey that consultants generally paid little attention to actively monitoring the cause–effect relationships of their various consulting activities to determine what performance improvements were attributable to or how performance could be improved. Average chargeable hours could be dropping to as low as half of the actual hours worked, so the consultant stated average charge rate of approximately $128 per hour would in reality be more accurately reflected as $64 per hour, unbeknown to the client, who thinks that on average they are paying the rate of $128 per hour for the work to be done. Neither the client paying the average $128 per hour fee, nor the consultant, who in reality is grossing $64 per hour (at the stated rate of $128 per hour), is benefiting from such a situation, where the true work input and value of effort is being underestimated by such a significant degree.

While setting 'benchmarks' for consultants, in terms of ethics, quality assurance, professional indemnity and public liability insurances, is both desirable and feasible, the range and average charge rates are less able to be standardised or benchmarked, because of the nature of a consultant's work.

What is however important is that consultants need to regularly re-assess their chargeable time when quoting for work to be done. They need to ensure that they are more accountable for the actual hours they invest in securing and undertaking the work and that the tangible benefits to the client can be demonstrated. Failure to do so would result in the client not seeing the true work associated costs or the value adding component of the work undertaken, in terms of the final account.

Inherent in the approach of more accurately determining the real cost of work performed and demonstrating the level of value adding that transpires is that the end result promotes the consultant for future such work.

Therefore those who engage in price undercutting or grossly underestimate their chargeable hours effectively devalue the profession and end up working more for wages than at professional rates. Clients may perceive those who charge actual chargeable costs as being 'overpriced' and/or those who charge 'low rates' as not requiring any special skills or knowledge to undertake the work at the lower prices.

In addition to these results, a number of interesting general comments were made by the Western Australian consultant respondents, summarized as follows:

> While benchmarking for consultancy pricing is useful as a guide to industry standards, it does little to control the price-cutting that goes on, particularly in an economically tough market. There was also the issue of the difference in benchmarking between large and smaller consultancies, which was not clarified (unfortunately the survey was unable to identify any differences as there was insufficient data made available by the larger consultancies).

A number of consultants ran 'mixed practices' and were not reliant on consulting as their sole income. This indicated that the scope of the questionnaire was less representative or relevant to them.

The question of 'good business ethics' came up, with the citing of some consultancies making use of subcontractors (students) who may not have the relevant expertise. Generally however the data gathered did not support the premise that subcontractors were used extensively by consultants except possibly where particular expertise (which the consultant may not have had) was required.

Determination of client satisfaction, the 'what and how measured?', was considered important, not only for benchmarking purposes but also for evaluation, marketing and repeat/new business reasons. Follow up reviews were needed to ascertain—were forward milestones met?, were changes required?, would they do the project the same way again?, were value expectations by client and consultant achieved?.

The reputation and standing of professional bodies was important, particularly as a reference point for consultancies considering overseas assignments and looking for professional recognition through association with these bodies.

The structure, pricing and type of consulting operation run by consultants were very much a sign of the lifestyle approach being sought and were not necessarily directly correlated to the market supply and demand situation.

What respondents would have liked to have had reviewed or included in the survey were issues such as the source and selection of new consultants, mixed practice to sole consulting practice comparisons, large to small practice comparisons, what consultants would do differently in their practices to achieve higher value outputs, office versus 'at home' consulting practices, impact of new technologies on small consultancies and particular 'start up' consultancy problems.

A number of the issues raised by the results of this survey are discussed in later chapters.

Relationships with clients

THE NATURE OF THE CLIENT–CONSULTANT RELATIONSHIP

The most critical component, and the most intensely intangible element, of consulting services is the client–consultant relationship. It is convenient to think of consultancy as being a two-way relationship between consultant and client—an approach I take in this chapter. However, in reality it is a relationship between two institutions or systems, which have groupings and hierarchies and multiple interests on both sides. In all I say about clients and consultants in the relationship context, it is well to remember that they are representatives of systems and therefore the relationship cannot operate without due consideration of the multiple interests of both.

It is clear that the consultant and client are inextricably linked in the context or milieu in which they operate, and a consultancy is not possible without the involvement of each. I see the two roles presenting a mirror image of each other, in terms of activities and characteristics, as shown in Figure 1.

It is worth noting that if you are a consultant, you cannot exist without a client, but a client can exist without you—a strong motivation to ensure that your selling skills are not neglected.

While the proposal or brief initiating the consultancy is an attempt to establish the basic parameters of the relationship in terms of tasks, authority, responsibility and communication, it is severely limited in defining many of the more subtle aspects of the

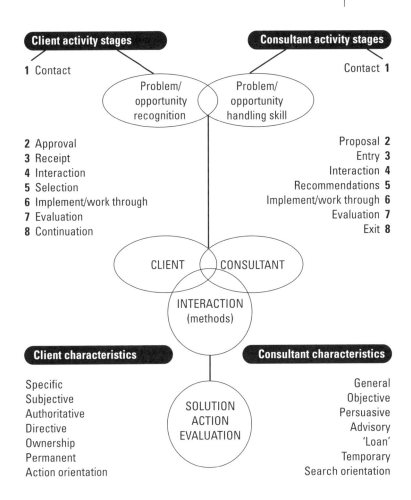

Figure 1 The management consultant's milieu

relationship. In simple terms, one could say that 'who pays the piper calls the tune', but the client authority inherent in a consulting relationship is quite different to that in a management role.

The models noted in chapter 2 are based on different premises in regard to this relationship. In the purchase model, the consultant is technical/topic/resource expert. In the doctor–patient model, the consultant is therapist/expert. In the process model, the relationship is based on the notion that business issues can be dealt with most effectively by linking the consultant's specialized skills with the client's knowledge of the situation in a collaborative way—thus process becomes as important as task. This approach is different to the traditional view that consultants analyse and recommend and clients decide and implement.

It is my contention that process consultancy—a model based on behavioural science—should be used even when the purchase and doctor–patient models are used.

Despite this contention, I think that a consultant who uses any of these models should not try to make clients dependent on them but, rather, should work to transfer expertise to the client organization. In other words, you work yourself out of a job. It can be hard to accept the idea that at the peak of your success, you become redundant!

THE RELATIONSHIP FIT

It should go without saying that the client and the consultant must be compatible if an assignment is to have a reasonable chance of success. There needs to be a good fit between client and consultant in terms of beliefs regarding what the organization/business is all about, objectives, personality, and motivation/assignment interest.

This reiterates a point made in chapter 2: the consultant's product is as much about the consultant as it is about his or her service.

While I find that I usually have to work in a relationship in order to test compatibility, it is often possible to sense in early contacts whether or not I am going to 'get along' with a potential client. It is hard to refuse the chance of a contract, but my experience suggests that it is far better for all concerned that serious doubts regarding the relationship fit, on either side, be explored, and that if these cannot be resolved, the contract not be finalized. Incompatibilities discovered later in a job can be harder to resolve and require a great deal of human relations skill (usually on the part of the consultant) to work through in a constructive manner.

CLIENT ROLES AND EXPECTATIONS

From my perspective as a consultant, I see my role as being closely related to my concept of consulting as a professional role exercised from a base of a 'body of knowledge', an 'institute', and colleagues who identify with each other and the values, standards and ethics espoused by the 'institute'. That is, I identify with the role defined for me by my professional body and my colleagues.

My expectations of clients are consistent, on the one hand, in that I see them as collaborators in view of the process model I use, but variable on the other hand, depending on the roles I choose (or have chosen for me)—for example, teacher, monitor, barbarian, expert. However, problems can occur if my client's expectations differ from mine, and this can most easily occur when the client wants me to be an expert with the answers—a role that I avoid on principle.

Consultants place those who pay them in the 'client' role, and use this generic term to describe them. But clients do not necessarily see themselves in this role. They identify themselves as businesspeople, scientists, public officials, managers and the like, and usually place a much higher priority on fulfilling this role than on fulfilling the consultant's expectations of the client role.

The client role, therefore, cannot be so readily defined, and nor can the expectations of people placed in that role by choice or by chance. For example, while I may well see everyone I interview in an enterprise as a client, it is highly unlikely that each interviewee sees him/herself in the same way. They identify with their job title and role, and thus their expectations of a consulting contact could range all the way from trust and hope to outright dislike and cynicism.

While it is hard to be specific about expectations, it *is* possible to make two generalizations:

- Clients generally do not want to be made to look foolish or incompetent or stupid, or to lose face.
- Clients are usually concerned with maintaining (or increasing if possible) their power and influence.

Both expectations can block consultant and client learning if they become the focus of the relationship, instead of what is expressed in the proposal.

At a national IMC conference in Queensland in 1998, a group of users of consultants who presented a session on partnering with consultants suggested that consultants consider the following points to increase their chances of success in such partnerships:

- Know what the project is all about—joint confirmation of the terms of reference.
- Follow the terms of reference, but also use initiative, creativity and flexibility as required.
- Treat our people as skilled and knowledgeable—don't be patronizing.
- Avoid prescriptive solutions.
- Be vigilant in use of language—gender-free, no jargon.
- Generate trust and open communication.
- Use the best people in the early design phase.
- Market and build networks within the organization.
- Work with people, not against them.
- Offer a competitive price.
- Research the operational environment.
- Extend/transfer skills to our people.
- Add value to our organization—that is, help our managers to do a better job.
- Focus on achieving outcomes/solutions.
- Have a meaningful performance reporting system.
- Help to unleash some enthusiasm.
- Help us to use you better.

People may become clients because they are feeling a 'pinch', a 'pain' or a problem, but usually they become clients because someone higher up decides that they need help. The call for consulting assistance is a top management decision to be carried out at lower levels. It is not often that top managers feel sufficient 'pinch' to hire a consultant to help them personally: after all, if one is at the top, it is because one is competent and many steps ahead of the pack. 'If there are problems, it is because of other factors besides myself' is a typical thought pattern of chief executives.

In this role, those chosen to 'host' a consultant learn to play the game, go along with the consultant, and show interest but move slowly enough to create no threat to a project.

Clients become clients for many reasons and not necessarily because they are ready to be clients. However, this is a fact of consulting life and should not prevent a consultancy from succeeding. With the passage of time, a consultant can work to create trust, and clear the air if necessary, to ensure that client resentment and resistance do not prevent the positive results that can be obtained by cooperative effort.

The expectation that a positive result will occur is not always an assumption that can be made—the project has to be worked at by all parties in order for there to be a good chance of success. As I have suggested before, there are a number of reasons why consultants are hired, and it is not always to get a successful result, even though this may be a stated expectation in a brief.

Consultants invariably work on someone else's problems or opportunities—they cannot take them away, solve them and give them back. The client always retains ownership and therefore the responsibility for action.

Consultants are not miracle workers who can 'save' an organization from its problems. They have useful tools that may help, but ultimately it is the client who must decide and act.

Even if a consultant did work in the role of 'expert', where the expectation was that he or she would solve the client's problems, the expert would eventually have to leave. If the client were not self-sufficient at that stage, then the expert solution could result in more problems than the one it was designed to solve, with the client struggling to cope without help. This is the main reason for my belief in process consulting interventions, even for consultants who offer expert specialist assistance.

PERMISSION AND TERRITORY

Issues

Central to the nature of the client–consultant relationship is the point made very clearly and at length by Sam Barcus and Joseph Wilkinson (1995): consultants can succeed only in so far as clients give them permission to operate on their territory. The concepts of permission and territory are crucial to understanding the consulting process.

The first permission to be granted must be that given by the client to him/herself before he or she can give the consultant permission. In other words, the client must say, 'I am going to allow this consultant to enter my territory, even though I understand that it could well cause work disruption, personal dilemmas and upsets to the status quo'.

People do not always say what they really think and feel; often they will say what they think is expected of them and what will not 'rock the boat'. It is necessary for the consultant to get well beyond the initial permission stage and into a deeper relationship of trust, so that what a client really thinks and feels, rather than the 'half truth', is in fact what is communicated.

It is easy to lose permission and territory if you are seen to use information gained in a negative or 'respondent loss' way. Consultants should also be aware that when people ask for advice, they are not always prepared initially to divulge all the things the consultant needs to know. They permit themselves to give a little as a test of the consultant's reactions (negative, critical and uninterested, or positive, constructive and interested) and extend permission to proceed further if they feel that this is someone they can trust.

It seems, then, that there are a number of levels of permission and territory to go through before a consultant is trusted with the full story. Permission and territory, although inherent to some extent in the brief and the proposal, have to be negotiated and renegotiated many times with many people during an assignment.

I have found that the ability to generate a climate in which clients have the confidence and trust to open up on all issues of concern relating to the assignment is one of the most powerful tools in my kit. Each permission gives me a little more territory. How I use the territory gained will determine how much more I get. It is a similar process to counselling or to conversation guidance.

Strategies

The following summary of hints on how to gain permission and territory has been gleaned from Barcus and Wilkinson (1995), supplemented by my personal experience of process consulting, and provides a good general guide.

Communication cues and clues

Develop skill at offering conversational cues and identifying conversational clues. For example, your cues might be questions about costs, morale, training and productivity, or based on your own experience.

Their clues often involve words like 'I', 'me' or 'they', especially when associated with adjectives that stress worry, distress, despair and satisfaction.

Words like 'urgent' and 'critical', and phrases like 'who cares about that', are also useful indicators of the direction in which you should be providing cues (questions) to progress your territorial gain.

A useful rule about clues is that you should always be alert for what people say about themselves. This can give useful information about the person, the situation, and the impact that the situation is having on the person. And it is important to listen to both what is said and what is not said—attitude and body language can provide clues to messages that sometimes remain unspoken.

When people are saying nothing, it does not mean that they have nothing to say. If you are interested and ask the right question, they will open up.

Their agenda

Remember that you are there to help a client think more clearly, not to gather information for your own satisfaction. A consultant with a tight, preset agenda who enters into communication with a client cannot expect to be able to penetrate the client's facade: the client will perceive the consultant's agenda and unconsciously keep his or her facade in place. The aim is to get clients talking about themselves and their problems, and in the process gain any information or insight that adds value to the project.

Problem versus solution

Remain problem-centred on most occasions until you are sure that you have the correct diagnosis before you become solution-centred. Do this even if the client already has a solution (a training program, for example) or wants you to suggest a solution soon after a symptom is described (high labour turnover, for example). Clients are no less prone than consultants to this 'solution' syndrome. The temptation must be recognized and avoided at all costs.

It is appropriate to be solution-centred if it is clear that the problem has been satisfactorily diagnosed, the client does not want to spend time working on the problem personally and is prepared to pay someone else (an expert) to provide a solution. In line with my assertions about process consulting, however, an expert consultant would do well to remember that arriving at a solution is only a minor part of the project: implementing it is the real challenge, and here process skills are paramount.

Some personal diagnosis to verify a client's conclusion never goes astray, either, if you have time and permission to carry it out.

Reporting

Summarize or report frequently so that all concerned agree that what has been said and done is in fact what has been said and done. In my experience, this constant monitoring and feedback of communication is probably the main area neglected by consultants — myself included, unless I constantly remind myself of the need.

Focus

Concentrate on the client's problem or the main point being considered, and avoid seductive detours that are of interest only to you — the 'intellectual cul-de-sac', as it were. If you have a particular interest in quality control and the client is a good source of information on this topic, it is tempting to concentrate on specific discussions of quality control rather than on the focus of the project—which could, for example, be how to improve performance in the assembly section. Though quality control is no doubt a variable in assembly, it should not dominate over the others that are involved.

Dynamics

There are a number of dynamics related to territory that are worth keeping in mind. These are summarized as follows:

- *Scene dynamics:* People's behaviour is affected by the situation in which they find themselves. They feel safer on their territory. The setting chosen for an interview, for example, can often determine the outcome of the interview in terms of generating valid and useful information. I have often gained the most information from interviews conducted informally with workers in their workplace while the work was being done.
- *Time dynamics:* Make sure you are both in the same conversational time-frame—that is, the past, the present or the future. If you are talking about past behaviour and the interviewee is talking about the present, there is little chance that you will reach common ground.
- *Topic dynamics:* What you talk about will highlight differences or similarities in five areas: me, you, us, them (who are not present) and things (weather, equipment, files, procedures, etc.). It helps understanding greatly if the talk revolves around one area/agenda item at a time. A sound rule I use is to begin with generalities to break the ice and then get clients to talk about themselves and their role. They will usually provide enough of a guide to how they feel about me, us, them and things to give me a fair idea of what questions to ask to ascertain their true thoughts and feelings about the issue being discussed.
- *Competition dynamics:* Try for a win-win situation. It can be easy to slip into confrontation mode with a client, particularly

if they are predisposed in that direction to start with and you get frustrated with the consequent lack of progress. Patience, sincerity, tact and honesty are the best attitudes to exhibit in order to avoid entering into competition with a client.

There are, of course, times when it *is* necessary to say or do things that may upset a client, because pulling punches does neither of you any favours.

Whatever happens, you need to try to get the client 'moving' towards you rather than away from you or against you, even though there may be movement in both directions during the course of the meeting or the project.

In the process of consultation, agreement does not mean commitment and disagreement does not mean rejection. You need to turn agreement into commitment, and action and disagreement into consideration. These issues are revisited, in the context of client resistance to change, in chapter 6 (p. 71).

- *Facts and feelings dynamics:* Both the rational and the emotional aspects of the problem or issue need to be covered. This means treating opinions and feelings as 'facts' because they are facts to the client. If there is enough agreement between all the providers of opinions and feelings, then they may well be considered as true facts in dealing with the problem or issue.

Commitment

Keep your promises, both those in the proposal and those you make along the way. The client is, after all, buying a promise, and to renege on that promise or any others is a breach of your client's faith in you and a sure way to destroy the relationship.

The corollary to this, of course, is that *you must not promise anything you cannot deliver.*

BUILDING A COLLABORATIVE RELATIONSHIP

A collaborative or process model approach to consulting often results in repeat business. Collaboration is more likely to produce good results, and your results are more persuasive than words because they create the positive mind set in clients that is essential to building an ongoing relationship.

I have found that the foundation of the relationship is allied to how well I get to understand and appreciate my client's business and the issues of concern, and how well my client understands and accepts my role in helping to resolve the issues.

The issues usually relate to rectifying a deteriorating situation, improving a situation, or identifying and acting on new opportunities. There are five common elements to each of these situations:

- *Identification:* description/substance of the issue;
- *Scope:* people affected by and nature of the issue (closed versus open-ended);
- *Location:* organizational/physical units where the issue has been observed;
- *Intensity:* importance and impact of the issue;
- *Timing:* starting point, frequency of occurrence, current stability.

Issue resolution usually involves gaining information about the people, the policies and procedures, and the management style; determining the most desirable outcome; and then designing and implementing a solution developed from an analysis and diagnosis of the generated information that produces that outcome.

As mentioned in chapter 2, much of a consultant's work is aimed at discovering how the unofficial system works in relation to the official system. The essence of most information generation techniques is, in fact, to find out how people really do their work as opposed to how the job description or the procedure says they do their work. How to do this is the subject of chapters 6 and 7.

DIFFERENCES BETWEEN PUBLIC AND PRIVATE SECTOR RELATIONSHIPS

As a final comment in this chapter on client–consultant relationships, I think it is important to identify the nature of this relationship in regard to public sector consulting and private sector consulting.

Consulting to the public sector is big business but involves complexities, interest groups, stakeholders, time horizons, constraints and decision-making forces that make it different to the private sector, as is shown in Table 3.

Unless a consultant is aware of these differences, there is a good chance that a failure to adjust to the particular situation, be it public or private, will result in a failure to achieve the objectives and outcomes of the project.

Table 3 Private sector versus public sector—consulting issues

Issue	Private sector	Public sector
Identification of client	Clear or nearly clear	Difficult
Nature of client	Single person/small group	Many persons or groups
Client objectives	Relatively clear boundaries and targets	Multi-dimensional and complex, irregular boundaries
Methodology	Important, but often less so than results	Very important, especially consultation/facilitation
Constraints	Relatively few	Many, difficult to define
Accountability for decision	Personal/small group	Collective, large group
Decision-making	Based on objective commercial criteria	Political, value-based
Documentation, report	Not always important	Very important, a public document
Results	Generally measurable	Often not measurable
Evaluation	Informal	Formal and complex
Implementation	Almost immediate	Uncertain, depends on political will, resource allocation, etc.

Source: Kubr 1996, p. 424

6 How is it done?
The consulting cycle

PROBLEMS VERSUS SYMPTOMS

Most of the assignments I work on are initiated by a client who has a particular problem. This problem is usually expressed in the form of surface problems or symptoms (sometimes called performance indicators)—for example, rising costs, staff unrest, communication difficulties, customer complaints, low staff skill levels, management inefficiencies, structural faults. An examination of the symptom or symptoms is the first step of my intervention and constitutes the first stage of the consulting cycle. Working with the client in finding out the nature of the causal problem/s and coming up with a good workable solution forms the main activity of the intervention, apart from implementation—if a solution reaches that stage.

This is not to say that the symptoms should be ignored once they have been recognized as indicating that a more deep-seated problem exists. There is no doubt that the immediate effects of symptoms such as staff unrest, personal conflict or customer complaints must be tackled in the short term to ameliorate the unrest, resolve the conflict and deal with the customers, and this requires short-term *reactive solutions*. Even these should not be tackled, however, before investigation to some extent.

However, the real issue is to find out what is causing these symptoms to surface, and this involves an in-depth process that will result in *preventive solutions* that, in the long term, will help prevent the symptoms from appearing again.

The critical facts underlying many issues are usually hidden within a mass of related facts and feelings, and it takes time and effort to discover them. Unfortunately, many people find it easier to accept the quick and easy answers than to undertake the sort of investigation and analysis necessary to allow these critical facts to emerge.

Even the specialists who can be called on to begin at the solution stage (because they have the answer) would be well advised, in my opinion, to spend some time on ascertaining whether the client has correctly identified the problem area. Fact/feeling finding and analysis should be used to verify that both the specialist and the client are on the right track.

Thus, in simple terms, organizations typically have immediate short-term problems (symptoms) that are indicators of more deep-seated, long-term problems or issues, and both must be tackled in order to improve present and future operations. It is not so much a question of problem-solving as of causing the problem not to exist.

In fact, the purpose or outcome of the assignment should be to accomplish a turnaround so that the symptoms or indicators become positive rather than negative — for example, high accident frequency rates become low frequency rates, high costs become low costs, low profits become high profits, many customer complaints become few customer complaints, low morale becomes high morale.

THE CONSULTING CYCLE MODEL

The consulting cycle consists of symptom recognition, problem finding and analysis, problem definition, setting of desired outcomes and objectives, solution generation and choice, solution and action plan implementation, and evaluation.

I call what I do a cycle because it is not necessarily a step-by-step methodology. Each part of the cycle is related to every other part, it is possible to work on one or more parts at the same time, and it is often necessary to go back to a part that was previously considered completed. I also call it the 'consulting cycle' rather than 'consulting process' in order to differentiate it from process consulting, where the term 'process' is used to describe the way in which the parts of the cycle are carried out—that is, in a collaborative and helpful mode rather than an expert mode.

I take the reductionist view that an understanding of the parts will give an understanding of the whole, although I recognize the validity of a holistic view of the cycle. With this in mind, the parts of the cycle are described in more detail later in this chapter.

A problem exists when there is a gap between expectations and reality. The real purpose of an assignment is to make changes that result in reality matching expectations more closely.

I use the word 'problem' in the same sense as is expressed by the Chinese language ideogram for 'problem', which incorporates meanings of threat and opportunity. Thus whenever I use the word 'problem', it should always be read as being interchangeable with the word 'opportunity'. In fact, it is a good strategy to consider problems in a positive rather than a negative sense—that is, as indicators of opportunities to improve a situation instead of as obstacles or blocks to progress.

Because problems indicate that something needs to be done to remedy or improve a situation, the problem identification part of the consulting cycle is sometimes called 'needs analysis' and is often used as a description for the activities (similar to those described in this chapter) concerned with arriving at indicators for what needs to be done to improve individual, group or organization performance. Another commonly used term for this is 'diagnosis' (see p. 63).

The components of the consulting cycle model I use—shown in Figure 2—are, in reality, similar to the problem-solving or decision-making steps featured in management texts. However, I have focused the task on the core component: the desired objectives and outcomes. From the top, or beginning, is the *problem analysis and synthesis phase*, when the task is to determine the problem/s, arriving at the *core phase* of determining objectives and outcomes. From the bottom, the *solution generation and implementation phase* aims at achieving the objectives and outcomes. The *evaluation phase*, of course, determines the success or otherwise of the whole cycle.

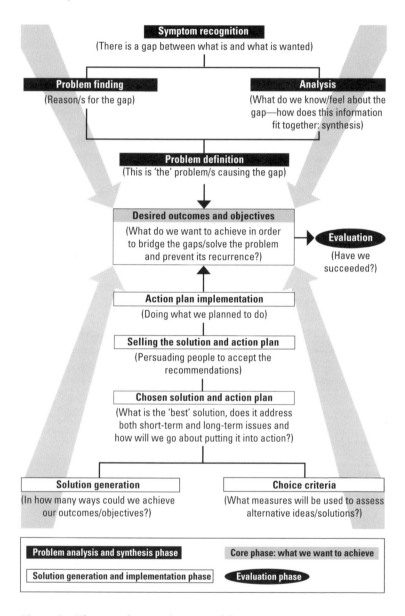

Figure 2   The consulting cycle—a model

PROBLEM ANALYSIS AND SYNTHESIS PHASE

Symptom recognition

Nothing can happen until there is the recognition that something is amiss. Clients must be aware that 'the shoe is pinching' and be prepared to act in a purposeful manner—either on their own or with consulting help. Typically, managers see symptoms as problems, and spring to the attack in a knee-jerk reaction. Consultants must remember the aphorism (discussed in detail in chapter 10) that problems are hardly ever about what they seem to be about. For example, rising costs may be the symptom or indicator of one or a number of causal problems. Also, one core problem can be causing many different symptoms. As noted earlier in this chapter, turning around the symptoms or indicators from positive to negative is the purpose of the assignment.

As described by Barcus and Wilkinson (1995), symptoms of problems (and therefore the problems themselves) have a number of dimensions, as follows:

- *Time dimension:* How long has the symptom existed, how much longer will it persist if left alone, how frequently is it likely to occur in future?
- *Frequency/intensity dimension:*
  - low intensity–low frequency (inconsequential)
  - high intensity–high frequency (immediate action)
  - high intensity–low frequency (monitor—dilemma)
  - low intensity–high frequency (annoying)

    The 'immediate action' reaction noted above is usually the main motivator for managers to hire consultants if they feel that they do not have the resources to take action, or that other dimensions of the situation (time, location, human, for example) suggest that a consultant would be more able to tackle the issues than internal managers.
- *Location dimension:* Is the symptom located in one spot or department or is it organization-wide?
- *Human dimension:* Are people concerns such as attitudes, tenure, pay, training, personalities and climate involved?

- *Support system dimension:* Does the symptom relate to equipment, policy, procedure or working conditions?
- *Tracking system dimension:* How was the problem/symptom detected (feedback control information, ad hoc method, observation, 'feel', etc.)?
- *Institutional problem managing dimension:* Is there a formal proactive method for handling problems or is it done informally in a reactive manner?

It was noted at the start of this chapter that another term for symptoms is 'performance indicators'. It is these that managers traditionally use to monitor and control the work of an organization, and they are closely related to the tracking system dimension. That is, if an organization has a formal tracking system, it is usually based on performance indicators, which are used to flag problems with the system when standard expectations are not met.

Problem finding and analysis

Facts and feelings are threads that run through the fabric of the consulting process. They are so important that a consultant must be competent in gathering facts-and-feelings information and skilled in its analysis. Associated with this activity is the attempt to establish reasons for the surface problems (symptoms). I approach this activity using the 'why' system—that is, why are the symptoms, which are so obvious, happening? It can be seen as a reverse tracking approach. If 'A' is the symptom, we ask why? If 'B' is causing 'A', we ask why? If 'C' is causing 'B', we ask why? We have found the basic cause or fundamental problem when the 'why' question has no answer.

This process is Socratic in nature and similar to the Theory of Constraints (TOC) method used by Eli Goldratt (1990). According to TOC, there is at least one constraint on every system—otherwise companies would be making infinite profits.

Such constraints, in TOC terms, are the fundamental or causal problems noted in the 'why' system. TOC uses a method of mapping out logical chains of 'cause and effect' relationships on paper—diagrams that are called 'trees'. The first tree, the 'current reality tree', is designed to answer the question: what's the core problem? It does this by visually depicting the existing undesirable effects—or symptoms of the problem—and then using known cause–effect relationships to find the very few, usually one, underlying root cause—the core problem. (Goldratt goes on to use the term 'future reality tree' to describe the mapping of solutions and their validity, and the term 'transition tree' to describe the implementation plan.)

The sources of such information to be analysed can be *internal* (corporate plans, organization charts/descriptions, marketing, manufacturing, financial and personnel data, and staff themselves) or *external* to the enterprise (industry reports, customers, competition, distributors and suppliers).

The type of information generated can be classified into quantitative and qualitative, although the boundary can become blurred when one attempts to classify a particular piece of information as one or the other. *Quantitative information* is tangible, objective and measurable, and is usually represented by facts and figures. *Qualitative information* is relatively intangible, subjective and immeasurable, and is usually represented by feelings, beliefs and opinions. As discussed later in this chapter (see p. 87), the ways in which these types of information can be analysed are substantially different.

In the generation of internal information, a consultant must be careful not to overlook the obvious and not to accept without question that what is stated on a document or said by a staff member represents reality. For example, a figure that appears on a document will have the appearance of fact, but that is no guarantee that it has not been distorted or treated in some way for public consumption. Compilers of 'facts' are not value-free. Similarly, feelings are facts to the people who express them, and people can be the most important source of information you have available. While it may appear to be a cynical approach, I have learned from bitter experience that nothing can be taken for granted.

The secret to getting at the true picture is to 'triangulate'—that is, to gather information from as many sources as possible and then compare and contrast it to arrive at what appears to be the generally agreed set of facts and feelings. This putting together of a clear picture from the array of varied and often conflicting information involves the application of synthesis—placing things together that seem to belong together.

There are a number of information generation techniques available to a consultant, and I usually use most of them on any particular assignment. They involve information gained from primary sources such as people and the situation itself by means of interviews, questionnaires, surveys, process studies and observation; and information gained from secondary sources such as organization charts, job descriptions, policies, procedures manuals and reports. Secondary information is based on document search, and this is the name often given to this technique.

These techniques are described later in this chapter (see p. 79), along with hints on how best to use them.

Problem definition

This is the end result of the information generation and problem finding process, when analysis and synthesis finally lead to a diagnosis. After information in the form of facts and feelings and opinions has been collected, analysed and synthesized, possible causal problems are identified and investigated and a decision is finally made on the real underlying problem/s. It is worth adding here that it is highly probable that more than one problem is at the bottom of poor performance—although, as TOC suggests, such constraints will be few in number. It is well to remember that a single core problem can manifest itself in a large number of symptoms.

Using a process consulting approach will ensure that the client knows what is going to be the outcome of analysis and synthesis, and will have been convinced of its accuracy before being faced with the final picture.

As discussed at the beginning of this chapter, it is usual to find that surface symptoms or problems that can be tackled in the short term are indicators of deep-seated problems that require a long-term solution. Thus an inter-departmental conflict about allocation and use of resources may be overcome in the short term by immediate negotiation and compromise, but unless the underlying reasons for the conflict are identified and dealt with for the long term (reasons that could include lack of planning, insufficient resources, poor communication of objectives and roles, etc.), such resource conflicts are likely to appear again and again.

Much of the information generated in this phase will be useful in the later phase of producing feasible ideas and solutions, because problem finding can also be opportunistic. The activity also provides a chance for the consultant to get to know and understand the stakeholders and the politics of the situation.

Pitfalls of the problem analysis and synthesis phase

During this phase of the consulting cycle, consultants should watch out for the following typical pitfalls—some of which have been noted before but bear repeating:

- mistaking symptoms for the underlying problem, and treating them without further detailed investigation—that is, not bothering to go through the basic analysis phase of the cycle;
- accepting without question the opinion of others concerning the situation;
- assuming that the problem is a person. In my experience, systems are more often at fault than people;
- 'slaying the bearer of bad news'—confusing the medium and the message is not only a factor in mass communication;
- overlooking the fact that many symptoms can be generated by a single core problem;
- jumping to a conclusion/solution before defining the problem. It is a common knee-jerk reaction of managers and consultants to do this because it looks decisive and generates immediate action—both of which are seen in a positive light when an organization is faced with difficulties. The delaying of solution action while facts and feelings are investigated is seen as procrastination and inaction—'pussyfooting'—consuming time and money without producing results! *Remember, all too often we find what we go to find.*

Succumbing to these pitfalls leads many managers and their organizations to try the latest management panacea, and there have been plenty of these over the years—for example, management by objectives, quality circles, organization behaviour modification, management leadership grid theory, job enrichment, self-managing work teams, and empowerment. The Americans call this 'cookie-cutter consulting'. If you already have the answer, then there is no need to go on to the solution generation stage of the cycle.

Another not so obvious trap for the unwary is *organizational overlearning*. Overlearning occurs when the organization develops an identity or competence in dealing with the external world that makes it blind in terms of its ability to deal with internal issues. For example, an organization whose primary mode is competitive and which needs to keep competitors guessing is likely to have internal competition as a process problem, which it will not recognize as a problem.

The organization that must react rapidly to a changing environment tries to make internal changes as rapidly—and internal change is much more difficult to get accepted. Externally, customers drive change and they want it; internally, managers drive change and others usually resist.

Many managers and peers censure members for raising issues about which decisions have already been made, particularly if those decisions were controversial. The questioners are seen as being negative and troublemakers. However, if the cost of re-examining old solutions is high, then systems will be slow to sense when old learning is no longer valued.

Diagnostic model

A model of the diagnostic process for examining organizations is presented in Table 4. It is only one of many such models but does identify the necessity of looking at the three major components of performance—the individual job, the group and the organization itself. Most change programs have to consider all three components if change is to be successful.

Important aids to diagnosis can be found in the various frameworks available to consultants. These include SWOT (company

Table 4 Diagnosing organizations—a model

Area	Inputs	Design components	Outputs
Organization	Strategy Task environment	Technology Structure Measurement systems Human resource systems Culture	Organization effectiveness, e.g. market share, return on investments, environmental impact
Group	Organization design	Task structure Composition Performance norms Interpersonal relations	Group effectiveness, e.g. quality of decisions, teamwork, cohesiveness
Individual job	Organization design Group design Personal characteristics	Skill variety Task identity Task significance Autonomy Feedback on results	Individual effectiveness, e.g. quantity and quality of performance, absenteeism, job satisfaction, learning, personal development

strengths and weaknesses, environmental opportunities, and threats), financial ratio analysis, cost/benefit analysis and the McKinsey 7-S framework (structure, strategy, systems, shared values, skills, style, staff).

CORE PHASE

Desired outcomes and objectives

Up to this point in the consulting cycle, we have been dealing with a negative—a problem (or problems). From here on, we need to change mind set and become positive, by restating the problem in terms of what has to be done to overcome it—that is, now that we know what the problem is, we can state an objective or outcome that, if it is achieved, will fix the problem.

Take, for example, the scenario in which the problem (symptom) is that the accident frequency rate in packaging and distribution is too high at 75. This is because of two main causal problems:

- a failure by maintenance workers working the out-of-hours shifts in the area to follow the safety procedures set down;
- an inadequate allocation of financial resources to the packaging and distribution section to enable them to acquire the necessary machine guards and safe handling equipment.

Our objectives in this case are:

- to make the packaging and distribution section aware of its accident frequency rate and its comparison to other sections of the company;
- to ensure that the out-of-hours maintenance shift workers follow the established safety procedures;
- to provide sufficient financial resources to the packaging and distribution section to enable it to purchase and install the machine guards and handling equipment needed for safe operations.

The first objective is concerned with the short-term or symptomatic problem and demands a short-term solution, while the second and third are concerned with the long-term problems and demand a long-term solution.

The outcome we want to achieve through meeting the above objectives is a frequency rate of 25 by the end of the next six months, without a decrease in productivity and with savings made through a lower accident frequency rate paying for the implementation of the solutions.

Note that with sound analysis, the objectives flow naturally from the problem/s diagnosed and described. The outcome is related to the original performance indicator of accident frequency.

With a set of objectives and an outcome clarified, we can then proceed to the next phase of the cycle: solution generation and implementation.

SOLUTION GENERATION AND IMPLEMENTATION PHASE

Solution generation

Having now determined objectives and an expected outcome, the focus changes from 'How do I overcome the problem?' to 'How can I achieve the objectives and thus the outcome?'—a much more positive approach.

The solution or 'deliverable' can vary from a report or training program design, to a systems design and implementation, organizational development program or counselling assistance. Whatever the solution, even when it involves changes to equipment, systems, policies, procedures or structures, it is not unusual to find that an educational or training component is needed.

Solution generation is perhaps better described as ideas generation. This is because most solutions end up being a combination of ideas rather than the result of a process recommended by the academic texts. These texts usually suggest that the problem solver come up with three or four unique solutions, which are then compared with the choice criteria, the one with the best fit being the one chosen.

In my view, however, we are engaged here in a creative process that involves, for example, bisociation (of ideas), and pattern recognition and matching through the use of techniques such as brainstorming, SCAMPER (substitute, combine, adapt, minimize or modify, put to other uses, eliminate, reverse) and morphological analysis.

There are many texts on creativity, learning organizations or organizational redesign/re-engineering that describe the methodology behind these and other techniques. Edward De Bono (1992) is a sound starting point for examination of the creative process and for ways of generating ideas.

The reason I present my consulting cycle model (Figure 2) with problem finding and solution generation both beginning from a broad base, and narrowing down to the objective or core of the whole exercise in the middle, is to escape the step-by-step sequence typically presented, and to indicate that both analysis/synthesis and creativity/solution generation require a broad mind set in application before a focus can be achieved.

The ideas themselves can then be sorted, evaluated, eliminated and combined in a variety of ways to produce one or more solutions, which can then be measured against the choice criteria and what needs to be achieved. Solutions should be as clear and understandable as possible, because consultants know from experience that complicated solutions rarely sell and, even if accepted, rarely work. Keep in mind the 'principle of parsimony' proposed by thirteenth-century Franciscan monk William of Ockham. This principle, which became known as 'Ockham's razor', says, in essence, that one should not offer complicated explanations or answers when simple ones will suffice.

The generation of alternative solutions is recommended, because only by comparison of solutions can you be sure that your final choice is, in fact, the best—that is, that it satisfies the criteria and will achieve the outcomes and objectives. Furthermore, clients often want to see that you have considered other solutions and may sometimes prefer one of the alternatives you have rejected; if this happens, the alternative they accept has more chance of being implemented than your choice, and it is probably better not to try to force your opinion. However, this sort of problem should not occur if a process consulting approach has been used, because the client will have been a part of the cycle activity and therefore a party to the solution.

Choice criteria

In order to evaluate solution alternatives, choice criteria need to be established.

These usually involve some form of cost/benefit analysis, with financial models (for example, net present value, break-even, internal rate of return) often playing a role if the overall company performance is being examined, or involving techniques such as decision trees and computer simulations if strategic decisions are being developed.

Generally it is cost, quality, quantity, time, legality, technical/operational feasibility, safety and employee satisfaction/morale that figure largely in choice decisions. However, sometimes, regrettably, personal whim may prevail.

While qualitative problems do not submit easily to quantitative criteria, it is usually still possible to put time and cost numbers to the objectives resulting from investigating such problems.

For example, if a solution to a customer problem is seen to be the production of a brochure, then an objective may incorporate the previously established criteria of a specified time for action and a maximum cost for such action in the following manner: 'to produce a customer service brochure before the next sales meeting within a budget of $5,000'. The final indicator of success would probably be related to the symptom that initiated action — customer complaints, in all likelihood. Evaluation of results is discussed later in this chapter as the last phase of the consulting cycle.

Another sample objective, if the solution involved communication, could be: 'to improve communication within the organization by holding monthly meetings with all department heads and quarterly meetings with all staff, to keep people informed of company performance'. The criterion of time in this example may have been as simple as specifying that the chosen solution should involve action within a month.

In the accident frequency rate example given earlier (see p. 64), the choice criteria are built into the outcome desired, in terms of frequency rate, productivity, time and cost.

Chosen solution and action plan

The solution chosen should be the one that gives the best fit or value relative to the established criteria. However, it is sometimes difficult to be certain of a good match.

For example, some important factors cannot be quantified, even at the 'one step removed' level noted in the brochure and communications examples above, or fitted into a known decision model, and criteria may be in conflict (for example, cost and safety — a dilemma called sub-optimization). A degree of uncertainty pervades the whole process, however much we try to pin things down with certainty.

Using the concept of degrees of certainty (uncertainty, risk/ probability and certainty), consultants usually operate in the risk/ probability area, with a bias towards uncertainty.

When the choice of solution is made, an accompanying action plan must be designed so that the client knows not only *what* is recommended but also *how* the solution is to be actioned.

It should be repeated, however, that it is highly unlikely that some thought to actions and the possible implications of actions will not have already been considered during the stages of generating ideas and solutions and establishing choice criteria. While I have compartmentalized the cycle to aid in describing it, it should be clear that it is a much more iterative, holistic and complex process than a straightforward sequence of steps.

The action plan—which might also be called a business plan, a project plan, a marketing plan, a corporate plan or a strategic plan—must be designed to show inputs, outputs, timing, budgets and organizational/personnel responsibilities in a clear and under-standable fashion for presentation to the client. The use of charts, diagrams, spreadsheets and other visual aids can be valuable presentation tools.

If the consultant has not already been using a process approach that involves the client at each step of the way, this is the time when he or she will have to start enlisting the client's help. It is impossible to draw up realistic and feasible action plans without working with the client on resource availability (particularly people), timing, slotting new actions into ongoing activities, equip-ment requirements and so on. Clients must be involved in the planning process for plans to have any hope of acceptance and implementation.

In this part of the cycle, it is important that consultants do not lose sight of the 'big picture' while concentrating on the issues and concerns of the situation under review. Don't let quantitative methods blind you to the value of creative insights and good old-fashioned 'gut feeling'.

Selling the solution and action plan

The need for communication

The basic skills of communication are essential during all phases of the consulting cycle, but they become crucial when it comes to persuading clients, and those who will be affected by the solution, to accept the chosen solution and action plan. As noted above, it is easier to gain acceptance if a process approach is used, but the range of people affected usually extends far beyond the key 'clients' with whom you have been working.

Often, final acceptance can depend on people with whom you may not have had any (or very little) contact during the project—for example, the chief executive officer (CEO), or people from departments outside the focus of the project but who will be affected by the actions to be taken. For major change, the whole-hearted support of the CEO is a crucial factor in organizational acceptance.

Reports and presentations

Formal reports and presentations take over as the visible manifestation of all the hard work done during the project, and unless they are of high quality and influential, all that hard work can count for nothing in terms of producing change and improved performance. You will probably get your money, but it will be grudgingly given and your reputation will not be enhanced.

There are plenty of texts on how to write reports and how to make effective presentations, and I do not intend to cover all that ground here. But a few simple pointers might help to stimulate interest in following up these matters in more detail.

For written communication, we are advised to analyse the audience, determine the purpose of the message, and organize it using a proper style in terms of tone, simplicity, precision, informality and conversational English.

While there is no standard format for consulting reports, they usually contain an executive summary; an introduction; sections describing what and how information was gathered and analysed to define the problem/s, the solutions considered, and the chosen solution and its recommended action plan; a conclusion; and relevant appendices.

Consultants are involved in a variety of oral communication settings, including conducting interviews, leading problem-solving conferences and making presentations. The more formal of these—oral presentations—are usually as much feared by consultants as they are by the managers who sit through them. As an audience, managers often receive a consultant's presentations in a negative frame of mind, since they have sat through similar presentations before and know that the usual standard is not renowned for being high.

I find that if I, as a presenter, can give them something they do not expect—that is, a stimulating, challenging and sensible presentation that enables them to say (covertly), 'He is describing us and our problems, he understands us, and what he suggests we do to improve makes sense and I'm all for it, even if it creates waves'—then we all stand a reasonable chance of winning.

The keys to success are:

- Prepare (know the audience, your purpose and your presentation plan).
- Practise if you can.
- Give an attractive, stylish and substantial presentation.

Some hints on how to do a good job of it are:

- Relax.
- Be optimistic and enthusiastic—don't apologize!
- Speak loudly and slowly.
- Use an outline and your visuals to guide what you say (don't read notes verbatim).
- Avoid fillers such as 'OK', 'right', 'ah', 'um', 'you know', and 'all the rest of it'.
- Use a conversational tone.
- Use gesture for emphasis.
- Use proper body movement/posture.
- Maintain eye contact.

- Vary pace and volume.
- Don't let visuals/technology become the focus of attention rather than you, unless you use a video or short contributing film; if you do, introduce it and then debrief your audience when it is over. The latest technology, such as Powerpoint, needs careful control so that style does not overpower substance: 'eye candy' can get in the way of a message!
- Use humour in good taste, and not at the audience's expense.
- Stop on time.

Client resistance to change

To end this section on a more complex but probably more realistic note, it should be kept in mind that agreement to a plan does not necessarily mean that it will be followed.

Once again, as the Glacier Metal Company experiments showed and subsequent research and experience have confirmed, the fact that much behaviour is governed by unconscious factors means that people are often unaware of many of the basic reasons they behave in the way they do. It is these multiple beliefs and motives, both conscious and unconscious, that give rise to the commonly observed inconsistencies of human behaviour. Stated policies or agreements to act are not always easy to carry out in practice, no matter how strongly they are consciously endorsed and believed in.

The message, then, is this: *do not assume that agreement in the selling session means a clear run in implementation.*

Consultants are also agents of change, and thus familiarity with the nature of change and the forces at work that assist and resist change should be a necessary part of the consulting tool kit.

While 'What to change?' and 'What to change to?' are technical questions, there is no doubt that 'How to cause change?' is a psychological one—and anyone who thinks we can overcome an emotional resistance to change by using logic has probably never had teenage children (Goldratt 1990). Emotional resistance can only be overcome by a stronger emotion, such as having some sense of ownership of the change as a result of contributing to the change decision and process.

Returning to the Glacier Metal Company project, the researcher–consultants made three assumptions that I believe consultants should assume today—and in future:

- The particular problems complained of were unlikely to be the only—or indeed the main—sources of difficulty.
- No simple causes or easy solutions would be found.
- Although assistance was sought, resistances to change were likely to occur as the real situation was further explored.

I have adopted this as my consulting credo and it has not let me down yet, although it does cause difficulties when dealing with clients for whom the problem is obvious, the solution straightforward and resistance can be 'ordered' away.

Consultant Peter Block (1981) suggests the following ways in which clients may resist your ideas:

- by asking for more detail as a ploy to avoid reaching the point of having to accept or dispute information already presented;
- by providing excessive detail as another means of avoiding reaching a conclusion;
- by being too busy or finding it is 'not the right time', as a defence strategy;
- by appealing to the 'real world'—the client claiming that the consultant can never understand the problem because he or she is not part of what is 'really' happening in the organization;
- by expressing 'I'm not surprised'—the client suggesting that everyone knew all along, which detracts from the value of the project;
- by being confused and asking for more and more clarification, which is like asking for more and more detail to avoid reaching a conclusion;
- by a 'flight into health'—where the need for intervention has diminished because the problem seems to have gone away with the resignation of a staff member, or a sudden upturn in revenue. This phenomenon may occur when the client does not want to face up to the findings of the consultant.

Resistance is rarely personal, but when it occurs it can be presumed that it is evoked by the consultant and it is the consultant who has to deal with it. The keys to handling resistance are to recognize it and the form it is taking, to name it and bring it out into the open with the client, and to talk about it and resolve it with the client by mutual agreement. The worst thing to do is to ignore or deny resistance.

A consultant should be working at gaining trust and overcoming possible resistance to change from the very first meeting with a client. I think there is a useful message in a comment by Arthur Koestler (1959, p. 427):

> The inertia of the human mind and its resistance to innovation are most clearly demonstrated not, as one would expect, by the ignorant mass — which is easily swayed once its imagination is caught — but by professionals with a vested interest in tradition and in the monopoly of learning.

Action plan implementation

Involvement of the consultant

In my experience, the selling of a solution that has been set out in a report and tabled for client approval is more often than not the end of the project. To be actually involved in implementation in the type of consulting I do is not always inevitable. Anecdotal evidence suggests that probably not more than 50 per cent of generalist consulting projects include implementation. This is a pity, as an excellent report does not guarantee complementary action, particularly if the client does not have the capability or determination to implement without help. This help can be given by a consultant in a number of ways, and does not have to be on a full-time basis with the associated costs that often prevent clients signing on a consultant for the implementation phase. The consultant could deal only with the more difficult parts of implementation; he or she could be 'on call' for the client; or the consultant could visit periodically to check progress. These low-cost options should be considered by clients so that the expertise they have worked with during the early phases of the project can be accessed when difficulties arise in implementation.

It is different if one is a specialist consultant and the task is putting in a new computer system or a new system of inventory control or quality control. In these cases, the client sees implementation *as* the project and has no qualms about involving the expert.

However, in generalist consulting, where the problems have to be identified, where top management is sometimes part of the problem, where so much may have to be changed to improve the situation and where such change is going to take a considerable amount of time and effort, clients often conclude projects at the report phase. This is sometimes known, rather facetiously, as the PRAPO (prepare report and pee off) effect.

In my view, consultancies that end in a report are more like research assignments. If the essence of consulting is initiating change and improvement, then a reports-only result can be a dead end unless it is expected as a 'research deliverable'.

Patterns and influences

Three key questions need answers if implementation is to occur:

- Who can? Who has the power and influence to get things moving?
- Who will? Who has the motivation to get things moving?
- Who pays? Every change has winners and losers, and knowing who they are (particularly the losers) can affect the strategy used to implement the change.

As noted earlier, major change is highly unlikely unless the CEO can and will get things moving.

Enterprises are dynamic, and each has its own particular pattern of structure, culture and personality. This pattern is continually being modified and developed due to the constant interaction of its components and the influence of the concurrent elements of power, authority, responsibility, communication, sanction, participation, cooperation, status rivalry, competition, dependence and dominance.

Patterns and influences make for a potent mixture in any enterprise and are the happy (or unhappy) 'hunting ground' of the generalist consultant who is trying to encourage change in the interests of improved performance. These patterns and influences affect the whole assignment, and so must be recognized as part of the consulting cycle, particularly if a process approach is being used.

The 'expert' does not always consider these patterns and influences, and may therefore wonder why his or her expert solution is undermined at the implementation stage when it has apparently been accepted by the client.

Although patterns and influences change, and the approved solution of yesterday can become the new problem for today because of such change, as a general rule clients can more easily see the pain that will be part of the proposed change rather than the possible gain—which is often only based on faith that the process of getting to a solution has produced the right solution.

It is worth remembering that solutions will always result in two sets of consequences—anticipated and unanticipated. As a consultant, you hope that the anticipated outcome is in fact the major outcome. However, the real world tends to yield unanticipated consequences that are more likely to be dysfunctional than functional. In other words, implemented solutions can create problems in unexpected quarters. Computer programmers know the dilemma well: they have a rule that says that every six lines of code fixed will generate one error somewhere else.

The role of reports

Many project briefs specify that the end of the project be marked by a report describing its progress, its results and its recommendations. However, when the report is left as the main proponent of the recommendations, when the few champions of change become deflected by the day-to-day concerns of the operation and when the client realizes the pain factor noted above, it is highly likely that not much will happen. In such cases, the report becomes history and remains in the bottom drawer.

Alan Weiss (1992) suggests that reports are often produced even when they are not requested, because consultants seek to follow the conventional wisdom that equates assignment end with report submission. Consulting seeks change, and a report in itself will not change anything: it is a means rather than an end in itself. Weiss also suggests that if a report *is* produced, it should be written by the client with the consultant's assistance, because it would then have much more chance of being accepted.

In fact, Geoffrey Hutton recommends that consultants never make recommendations (this point is discussed further in chapter 10, p. 130).

Timing

My most successful projects have been those in which I have been involved in all phases of the cycle, including implementation. True process consulting sees the consultant as the client's partner in the full cycle of performance improvement activities. This usually means client–consultant contact over a much longer period than is normally allocated to the production of a report.

While it is hard to be definite about timing, I have found that implementation of jointly agreed recommendations will take three to four times as long as it took to produce the recommendations. The tyranny of urgency often militates against managers implementing recommendations—even their own!

When working on a problem, I prefer to produce, along with the client (represented by a counterpart), a series of working papers that can initiate implementation activities as soon as possible and thus obviate the need for a final one-off report that marks an arbitrary cut-off between what has been happening and what is recommended to happen.

Hutton (1972a) calls this 'working through'—a term I like to use as a good operational description of process consulting.

Elements

There are some fundamental aspects of implementation that are basic to getting things moving, whether the consultant is involved or not. These project management points will be familiar to anyone who has had to get action of any sort under way.

Implementation can involve a pilot or a full run, but in either case the main elements—developing a work plan, and setting up controls, staffing and documentation—are the same. These elements are discussed in detail in chapter 7 (p. 99).

EVALUATION PHASE

Follow-up and evaluation of the implemented solution is the final phase of the cycle.

This is the point where results are measured to check whether the objectives and outcomes have been achieved, answering questions such as: did we meet our objectives in terms of the criteria established? Did the accident frequency rate reduce? Did morale improve? Did customer complaints fall?

It is important to note the difference between objectives and outcomes, because it is possible to achieve the former but not the latter. For example, in the accident frequency rate scenario given earlier (see p. 64), the objectives were:

- to make the packaging and distribution section aware of its accident frequency rate and its comparison to other sections of the company;
- to ensure that the out-of-hours maintenance shift workers follow the set down safety procedures;
- to provide sufficient financial resources to the packaging and distribution section to enable it to purchase and install the machine guards and handling equipment needed for safe operations.

The desired outcome was a frequency rate of 25 by the end of the next six months, without a decrease in productivity and with the savings made through a lower frequency rate paying for the solutions to be applied.

However, even if we succeeded in our objectives of raising awareness, following the safety procedures and installing equipment guarding, we might not achieve a satisfactory drop in frequency rate as an outcome.

Why might this happen? The obvious answer is that the problem has not been correctly identified; that some other factor or factors outside our perception are at work. The only option when caught in this dilemma is to start again—if you and the client can afford it! The message here is that the outcome is much more important than the objectives.

The process of evaluation has many similarities to the analysis phase that began the cycle, and could well lead to refinements and modifications of the solution implemented. If we have fallen well short of the desired outcome, it is necessary for us quickly to return to information generation and analysis/synthesis in another attempt to determine the basic cause of the poor performance indicator.

SUMMARY OF SKILLS REQUIRED FOR CONSULTING CYCLE PHASES

I consider the key skills needed for the main phases of the consulting cycle to be:

- *Problem analysis and synthesis phase:*
  - for problem finding and definition, *analytical* skills (and an ability to *synthesize* the results of analysis);
- *Solution generation and implementation phase:*
  - for solution generation and choice, *creativity*;
  - for action planning, *administrative* skills;
  - for selling the solution and action plan, *persuasive* skills;
  - for action plan implementation, *managerial* skills.

Thus the cycle requires a combination of skills, and any consultant who wants to use a process consulting method must develop these, underpinning them with an ability to deal with people both individually and in groups.

METHODS

This section deals with methods used by consultants to generate information and analyse/synthesize it prior to problem identification, as the effectiveness or otherwise of this component tends to be the principal determinant of a successful project.

Information collection

Interviews

Interviews are face-to-face meetings between two or more people, with the aim of exchanging information for a specific purpose.

Most of the information generation interviews that I conduct during the period of a consultancy are designed to obtain the views of the person or persons interviewed in relation to the particular issues that are the subject of the consultancy. They are not designed to obtain facts and figures that can be better extracted from documents.

I treat any meeting with people during a consultancy as an opportunity to gather information, whether I consider it important at the time or not. It is not unusual to find that valuable information can come out of the most casual of meetings.

Interviews can be formal and follow a set sequence of questions (an interview schedule), or informal and relatively unstructured. Each approach has advantages and disadvantages. The structured interview is easier to manage, and easier to analyse, particularly when you are considering a number of interviewee responses. However, because it is controlled by the interviewer, it can generate shallow information and not get at an interviewee's real feelings, as is possible during an unstructured interview. The unstructured interview is much harder to carry out and requires a high level of communication skill to produce the desired results. It is also much harder to record and analyse the information obtained in an unstructured interview, as there is no order involved, and particular topics can resurface on unexpected occasions during the course of the interview. Both types of interview can be held on a one-to-one basis or with groups.

Each interview type and situation is unique, and the interviewer must be prepared to react as necessary to keep 'contact' with the interviewee/s and ensure that the interview stays on track and generates useful information. However, I have found that most interviews can be improved by following these few basic steps:

- Learn as much as possible about the interviewee/s before the interview.
- Determine the purpose of the interview.
- Set out the interview guide/structure—for example, questions to ask or stages to follow or areas to probe.
- Schedule the interview time and location (usually an hour is a comfortable limit).
- Establish a friendly atmosphere early in the interview.
- State the purpose and structure of the interview—why it is happening, what will follow, who else is being interviewed, who is sponsoring it, how the information will be used (confidentiality is important), and what your role as consultant is.
- In conducting the interview, start with the interviewee's role, listen (to words and body language), and be objective and tactful. Give up the guide and play it by ear if you are not getting anywhere.
- End on a positive note, summarizing if needed.

I never use a tape recorder in my interviews, as I have found that it inhibits people, but there is no prohibition on using such recording means if it is done openly and is agreed to by the interviewee/s.

My method is either to take notes during the interview or to store the information in my head and record it immediately after the interview. I find that the latter method makes me concentrate and listen carefully to what is said (and not said), and I am able to monitor body language more easily. Interviewees tend to be more relaxed and open when one is not seen to be scribbling down their every word. I do not want to write down every word anyway, but rather to get the major points made and to record my impressions based on the interviewee's reactions and responses.

If I have any doubts about certain areas covered or cannot recall some points, I can always do a return visit or a phone follow-up—often a good idea anyway, as a second contact can uncover more information.

Group activities

There are a number of group activities that can be used for generating information, such as brainstorming, force-field analysis, Delphi analysis, focus groups and problem-solving conferences. These are the subject of considerable research, and there is extensive literature available on their methodologies. Rodney Napier and Matti Gershenfeld (1973) cover most aspects of group behaviour and working with groups, and this text is not outdated, despite its age. The subject is also covered in most books on organization behaviour and leadership.

Group work relies on sound preparation and planning by the leader, briefing of participants prior to the activity, management of the group by keeping it on track, and getting all participants to contribute without fear or favour in order to reach the outcome desired. The research of Irving Janis (1972) on 'group think' should be required reading for any consultant who works with groups.

As in any group meeting, it is essential that

- each participant is encouraged to contribute in a frank and open manner;
- assertive and verbose members do not dominate;
- status and position do not determine the value of comments and suggestions;
- hidden agendas and lack of trust do not detract from the objectives of the meeting.

A major part of the leader's job is to ensure that group process factors assist rather than hinder the task being tackled. According to Wilfred Bion (1961), a group will often look 'as if' it is working on a task when in reality it is bogged down in process issues such as dependency on the leader, 'fight or flight' in regard to the group, and pairing between like-minded members who find comfort in the resultant security. In all these 'as if' processes, the task tends to get ignored. Bion was the first director of the Tavistock Institute in the United Kingdom (see p. 11), which was set up to research the possible application of psychological and psychoanalytical theory to industrial issues.

As demonstrated by the Glacier Metal Company experiments, fear of looking at one's role and behaviour in the group, and of the group processes themselves, because this could release destructive forces that could damage the group, is a powerful disincentive to effective group work. It makes the job of a consultant keen on bringing these processes to attention and discussion in group situations very difficult.

Questionnaires/surveys

Questionnaires/surveys are documents produced to elicit responses from people on particular issues or topics in other than a face-to-face context.

This means that respondents usually receive them through a mailing system and respond as requested by the instructions that accompany them and according to the nature of the questions asked. Questionnaires and surveys stand or fall on the inclination of respondents to fill them in (response rates are often low), the relevance and clarity of the questions asked, and the care and honesty with which respondents answer the questions. When used for academic research pursuits, they are commonly called 'instruments'.

The questionnaire or survey is a restricted channel of communication and is thus best used to gather facts rather than feelings. However, because it is relatively easy to set up (although its ease can disguise the difficulty of structuring questions that are clear to respondents and will provide relevant and valid responses) and to analyse, it is a favourite tool of many consultants. It is also useful in that a large number of responses can be generated in a short time, from inside or outside the organization.

While certainly more efficient than interviewing, I have some doubts about the effectiveness of questionnaires or surveys, especially when used to measure feelings and views.

As with interviews, it is possible to suggest some guidelines that help to make surveys more effective:

- Use an accompanying letter to explain purpose and use of the survey, and the security of information generated.
- Give detailed instructions on how the questions are to be completed.
- Set a return deadline.
- Ask pointed, clear and concise questions.
- Format questions for ease of tabulation of answers (but be aware that ease of tabulation is not the purpose of the exercise!).
- Provide sufficient space for answers.
- Add space for extra clarifying comment on questions if needed.
- Identify each questionnaire with the respondent's name, title, etc. (unless anonymity is required or is likely to contribute to more truthful answers).
- Include a final section for further comment or opinion.

Observation and process study

Observation and process study includes listening and can also be accompanied by questions to clarify what is being observed and heard. Information gathered by this means can be done informally at any time during the course of a consultancy, or it can be part of an organized activity to check on how things are done in specific venues or sites, or it can occur during meetings with clients.

I find that valuable information abounds in the workplace. For example, it can be observed on bulletin boards and posted notices, inferred in the way people tackle tasks and move about the site, and illustrated by how facilities and equipment are placed and guarded.

Observation is a useful tool for consultants and can be used to gather general situational information or more direct information such as what is being done, how it is being done, who is doing it, when it is being done, how long it takes to be done, where it is being done and why it is being done. The 'why' is, however, not always clear unless some questions are asked.

It is useful for gathering facts prior to interviews, for verifying facts given in interviews and for determining relationships between jobs and people.

One can walk through an area, taking notes, observe secretly from a fixed location, observe openly from a fixed location, or observe and interact with the person being observed. Techniques for doing this in an organized manner include work or method study and other tools associated with process re-engineering.

My inclination is never to act in a secretive manner because it can destroy people's trust in me, and trust is one of my most valuable assets—without trust, I find that it is almost impossible to get a true picture of the client situation.

Again, as with any technique, preparation is necessary, particularly for organized observations. The following guidelines can help the observation activity:

- Tell people why you are there and what you are doing.
- Note the time at intervals during observation so that you can match actions to the time taken to perform them.
- Record what you observe as specifically as possible.
- Don't make value judgments when interacting.
- As soon as possible after observation, record your findings (although I am not averse to taking notes in such formal observation).
- Review your findings with the person/s observed and his/her/their supervisor.

If you are using standard work study approaches, then the process is well described in any number of books and manuals. Anyone familiar with work study will recognize such terms as 'process flow chart', 'string diagram', 'time and motion analysis', 'two-handed activity chart' and 'workplace layout map'.

You need also to be aware of the other side of the 'seeing is believing' catchphrase—that is, *believing is seeing*. Do not let your predispositions cloud your vision!

Observation is a vital component of any attempt to gain information, because it is such a vital part of the communication process. In any personal interactions, we not only hear what is said but we watch to see if the 'body language' and 'attitude' signals match what is said. Observation accompanied by our 'sixth sense' intuition enables us to put everything that is said to the sincerity test. Does the person really mean it?

This is also why, in my view, the interview is far more productive than the survey for getting at real views and opinions. You can make good contact with people in a face-to-face situation, while in a survey you do not see the person writing the answers and so do not have the advantage of being able to observe how they approach what they write. They may be sincere; they may not—but you have no way of knowing.

The final test of sincerity is whether actions match the talk. In Jaquesian terms (Jaques and Clement 1991), do people 'walk the talk'?

Document search

Document search is a non-reactive technique and can be done relatively easily, because it takes none of the client's time except that required to retrieve the documents.

An inspection and analysis of all relevant documents can give you valuable insights into what should be done, what is being done and how it is organized, as well as what the results are.

Documents can include structure charts, company history, job descriptions, procedure manuals, policy statements, financial returns, strategic plans, meeting minutes, training material, induction material and marketing brochures. Anything that has been written about the company, its people, the way it operates internally and in relation to outside stakeholders, and the results it has achieved and is obtaining is useful.

The main difficulty in generating information by this method is getting access to the documents themselves. Some could well be confidential, and many are scattered throughout the organization and so have to be accessed via a number of different people. I find it useful to specify in my proposal to a company that I will need access to certain named documents so that the client is not surprised when I request this during the consultancy (usually early in the cycle).

A request for documents is usually best included in the methodology section of the proposal but can sometimes be overlooked because it is not so obvious a method as interviews and surveys.

Intuition

Searching for information, or 'evidence' as I sometimes call it, does not always have to be carried out in a systematic manner. As Steele (1975) says, we often need to rely on intuition as a mode of operation. That is, it is useful to stop trying to control where you focus attention and let natural awareness lead you in whatever direction it will. In a sense, Steele suggests, you should stop staring at the information and allow the figure and ground relationships to shift around and take on new meanings or potencies. It is intuition that then enables you to understand what is seen as the eye and the mind roam over the situation.

Information analysis and synthesis

Pulling it apart and putting it back together

The next stage of the cycle is to analyse the information that has been generated. It is simplistic to assume that this process will not have already begun as soon as information begins to be collected. Hutton (1979) explains this by the aphorism 'Action begins where analysis begins' (see chapter 10).

However, I find that the thoughts, ideas and feelings that occur to me during this collection stage have to be played down to a large extent. There is no worse fate for a consultant than to prejudge issues or suggest causal problems on the basis of limited information. This can arise when you are working with an inadequate budget, or to a time schedule that is too tight, either of which may prevent thorough information gathering.

It is natural to think about information in relation to the issues of the project as it is collected, but it is dangerous to come to conclusions until information collection is complete.

Another warning here: although you may be in the final analysis stage, it does not mean that no more information can be gathered. It is not uncommon to have to go back to respondents or to documents to get further information or to verify findings during the course of analysis.

In my view, information analysis is accompanied, inevitably, by *synthesis*. It is impossible to analyse—the process of sorting, comparing, evaluating and eliminating information and categorizing it—without at the same time making decisions on the true facts and/or feelings in the situation, and synthesizing these into a composite picture that reflects as closely as possible the reality of that situation.

Finding the parts of the puzzle must be accompanied by putting those parts together again in a more comprehensible pattern. Analysis and synthesis are two sides of the same coin.

This pulling apart and putting together of information is no mean task and there are no set rules for doing it.

Quantitative information

Quantitative data tend to be easier to analyse than qualitative data, simply because numbers can more easily be coded and analysed by computer programs that have been especially designed for statistical analysis. Methods for such analysis/synthesis include charting (of jobs and relationships, system flows, etc., if not done already as part of a work study process), decision tables/trees, statistical analysis, input–output analysis and the many other quantitative tools that can be found in any book on management science and decision-making.

Not all quantitative information is capable of being handled by computer or algorithms, of course, but consultants (and researchers) usually attempt to use these tools whenever possible because of the credibility given to the results by those to whom they are presented.

Qualitative information

The term 'qualitative' applies to a wide range of information that is relatively unstructured and not conducive to being reduced to numbers.

Qualitative data analysis, often called 'content analysis', tends to lack the positivism of the orderly models and algorithms associated with quantitative analysis because it has to be heuristic in nature. I have to state, however, that the positivism of quantitative analysis is sometimes an illusion. The outcome depends very much on the quality and accuracy of the information fed into the computer.

Heuristics, as it relates to problem-solving, depends on inductive reasoning from past experience and similar problems, because there is no algorithm available for use. The process is active, direct and subjective, and the results are dependent on the judgment, experience, mind set and emotional reaction of the consultant to the project and to the people with whom he or she has interacted.

This is not to say that content analysis cannot be carried out in a systematic manner, but that the methods and the results will probably generate as much heat as light—particularly when questions of reliability and verifiability are asked.

The method has limitations, which relate mainly to the difficulty of handling qualitative information, and to analyst bias in seeking to provide an explicit rendering of the structure, order and patterns found among a set of participants in a particular situation.

In recent years, computer programs designed for analysing qualitative information have been developed. For example, a company in Melbourne operating out of La Trobe University, Qualitative Solutions & Research Pty Ltd,† is dedicated to the research, development and marketing of qualitative data analysis software and services. It offers two software packages, QSR NUD*IST4 (nicknamed N4) and NUD*ISTVivo (Nvivo). These packages are primarily intended for researchers but would be useful for consultants in circumstances where the data could be formatted in a suitable style.

A multi-level approach

A consultancy will often require the analysis of both quantitative and qualitative information, and so it is not a case of one type of information being better or worse than the other. The nature of the

---

† Email: help@qsr.com.au

consultancy and the circumstances in which it is carried out will determine the types of information that need to be gathered and analysed.

As I have suggested earlier, some synthesis will be taking place (perhaps unconsciously) during the analysis stage, but the final synthesis involves the consultant in putting the true facts and feelings together in such a way that they explain the problem clearly.

The objective of synthesis is to create a logical, ordered and understandable picture/pattern/problem definition from the usually illogical, disordered and apparently unrelated information generated and analysed.

I usually view problem finding and definition (or needs analysis, as it could be called) as a two-level process. At the first level, I am structuring a generalized objective picture of an enterprise, department or section, and determining by such general level analysis and synthesis a pattern or picture that identifies relationships, inputs, outcomes, operational procedures, problems and, perhaps, opportunities. This is a broad band socio-technical view of the system.

The second level of analysis and synthesis involves the in-depth examination of specific needs/problems within the classifications obtained in the first level. Thus I am deciding on the causal problem/s or core needs that must be addressed.

Whatever the methods used in this analysis/synthesis phase of the consulting process, an end result—a definition of the problem—will generally emerge. Hopefully, it will be correct, because a consultant's reputation is largely determined by whether or not he or she comes up with the real causal problem. Solutions directed at the wrong problems will cause continuing trouble for clients.

The best way of avoiding problems and surprises for the client is to use a process consulting approach in which the client participates, in one way or another, in all phases of the project and is informed about progress and results on a continuing basis.

How is it done?
Project management

WHAT IS A PROJECT?

A project is an activity that stands alone and apart from normal enterprise operations and has a definite beginning and estimated conclusion. While it is organized separately from the client's regular business activities, its progress and results will affect that business.

Projects are characterized by having specific expectations to be fulfilled, a set time in which to fulfil them and finite resources (including money) with which this must be done.

Because the nature of consulting projects varies so widely, the techniques of managing them must also differ to meet the particular circumstances.

Projects differ mainly in terms of deliverables (outputs of value to the client) and complexity. I would classify a short, straight-forward intervention involving only a day or so as a consultancy assignment, while I would call a more complex intervention over a period of weeks, months or more than a year a consultancy project.

Another type of consultancy that is growing in use in the United Kingdom and the United States is that of mentor to CEOs and senior managers—a so-called executive coaching consultancy. Executives are seeking this personalized help in order to assist them in coping with rapid promotion in organizations whose management layers have been pared to the minimum. Coaching with experienced consultants also gives them an opportunity to sound out ideas and be challenged in regard to how they do things currently. The sessions are usually of one to two hours' duration and can be spread over a period of weeks or months.

This chapter considers the project in some detail because it is a more difficult activity to manage than a brief or a coaching assignment. The latter require little or no project management skills, although they can have some of the elements characteristic of a project.

PROJECT INITIATION—CONSULTANT'S POINT OF VIEW

I consider that the proposal for a project is the first phase of the project management process. It is not only a sales tool that presents a professional and persuasive offer to provide assistance or service to a potential client; it also sets out the framework within which the project will be carried out, managed and evaluated.

Types of proposal

The most common types of proposal I write are in response to direct requests for proposals, advertised requests for proposals and unsolicited requests, usually from current clients. Requests for proposals or expressions of interest are commonly called briefs or given the shorthand nomenclature of RFP or EOI. Requests for tenders are usually headed as TOR (terms of reference). Many government organizations require consultants to be accepted onto a pre-registration list for contracting on consulting projects up to a certain amount ($50,000 is the amount usually nominated in Western Australia) and will only receive proposals from those they select from the list. For tenders over the nominated amount, an open request for responses is the norm.

If I feel uncomfortable with a brief, from whatever source, I do not usually respond. The briefs advertised by government (usually as RFPs, EOIs or TORs) tend to make the service appear as a commodity, and so the client tends to look at price rather than value. Responding to such public sector briefs needs careful research into the department concerned, which consultants it has used before and who is currently employed. Appointments are sometimes decided beforehand, and you may be going through the motions to satisfy a procedure, and thus spending an inordinate amount of time, money and effort on what is a lost cause from the outset.

If I do respond to these briefs, I follow the guidelines religiously because the bureaucratic mind will place negative judgment upon any proposal that shows initiative and puts things out of what it has considered as the logical order and requisite points to cover. I will sometimes put in an alternative method to that suggested, or add points I think are relevant to the project proposed, but I do so in the interests of my integrity and in full knowledge that it will probably be frowned on by the assessors.

Proposals to the private sector do not have to address the long and detailed requirements and conditions set by the public sector, which can issue briefs for consulting projects of up to twenty pages or more. Private sector briefs may comprise only a few pages describing the project itself, and the conditions under which the contract will be let.

The private sector proposal, while it often needs to include the elements listed below, can on occasions—particularly when dealing with a past or current client—involve simply a letter of understanding.

Characteristics of an effective proposal

An effective proposal should demonstrate *all* of the following characteristics:

- a client-oriented focus and an understanding of the client's problem/need that suggests that an easy rapport with the client in a climate of mutual trust will be established without difficulty;
- a realistic approach to the actions proposed to deal with the problem/need;

- an understanding of who the client's decision-makers are and their decision process in relation to the evaluation of proposals;
- an awareness of the overall business considerations likely to affect the buying decision;
- knowledge of the seriousness of the problem and the level of urgency in dealing with it;
- evidence of established credibility or reputation for providing the services offered;
- fees that reflect the value of the offer to the client.

Elements of a proposal

The main elements of a proposal are the same, whatever the project, even though the order and style of presentation may differ according to requester need or responder preference. It is better to have a unique approach to incorporating these elements into a proposal, because it serves to make it stand out from the efforts of other respondents. As noted above, this flexibility is not usually possible or advisable in proposals to the public sector.

These elements are:

- a description of *your* understanding of the problem or need defined by the client;
- a description of your approach and work/project plan (the methodology, activities, timing and resources, including any assistance or documentation required from the client);
- the results/benefits and positive outcomes/deliverables that will accrue to the client as a result of using you—estimate the financial returns, if possible;
- your relevant experience and that of your firm (make sure they match with the service being offered);
- the project staffing (who will assist and what their qualifications and experience are);
- any assumptions, qualifiers or disclaimers in relation to the project;
- fee arrangements—the total fee (and an itemized account of how it is made up), with a requested payments schedule.

The proposal cycle

The proposal cycle usually follows a pattern that consists of the following steps:

- The initial opportunity is presented via an advertisement, a personal call or a referral.
- Background research on the client and/or problem is carried out to put the opportunity into context.
- The client is contacted for extra information (and to establish recognition), by means of telephone, or an on-site visit and meeting, or participation at a bidders' conference.
- A decision is made on whether or not to pursue the opportunity by writing a proposal.
- If the decision is positive, a proposal is prepared (and an independent check of its content, style and selling value is useful).
- The proposal is presented, in person if possible, in order that the consultant may sell him/herself as much as the document.
- Follow-up contact is made within a reasonable time, to show interest and to ascertain whether the proposal has been either won or shortlisted (and is thus still in contention).

Selection or rejection

In the selection process, the four main factors likely to be used to judge the quality of a consultant, and to compare consultants if required, are (in no particular order):

- the quality of the proposal;
- the fee quoted;
- the consultant's 'fit';
- the consultant's reputation.

If the proposal is well written, logical and convincing, and shows a good understanding of client needs and expectations and a sound approach to the assignment, with the resources quoted matching the needs, it stands a good chance of being shortlisted.

If the fee, whether time-based or fixed, offers fair value for cost and is consistent with going rates, considering the nature of the assignment, it stands a better chance.

If the client feels comfortable with the consultant's personality and manner, and accepts (generally) the consultant's values and beliefs (perceptions gained from the proposal or pre-proposal meetings), things will look very good for the proposal.

Given the low barriers to entry to the profession, clients could look for membership of the IMC, as it is the regulatory body for consultants at this time (or membership of equivalent institutions for human resources management, information technology, etc.).

Reputation is often a major selection factor—and a solid reputation for good performance on previous jobs is a key determinant of quality.

Despite claims to the contrary, consultants suspect that many assignments (particularly public sector assignments) are won on a price basis. Clients often do not use the channels available upon which to judge consultant quality, and the easy 'out' is to consider that consultants are all capable of offering similar services to the same standard, and therefore the cheapest is the best.

Clients have also been known to use proposal information to do the assignment internally, so consultants should not 'reveal all' in their proposals.

Research in the United Kingdom (Keeble, Bryson and Wood 1994) suggests that the primary factors in a consultant's success in winning work are:

- existing relations with clients;
- reputation of the consultant;
- general image of quality;
- 'word of mouth' recommendation.

The past is used as an indicator of the future. Proposal/presentation quality and cost appeared at the bottom of the list! The implication of this research is that it is difficult for a new consultant to find and win assignments.

In summary, it pays to involve the client in your proposal, if you can, by having at least one meeting to discuss the brief or RFP and its terms and conditions, so that you can focus more clearly on client needs.

Your writing style should be consistent and the grammar and spelling accurate. Logic and clarity must be evident, and it's a good idea to avoid what could be called the 'glossy' syndrome, where attempts are made to obscure substance with glamour.

It can pay dividends to use graphics, because a picture or diagram is often worth one or two pages of words, but do not overdo it or your document could end up looking like a comic book!

The proposal is essentially a selling document and should appeal to the recipient from both a rational or utilitarian perspective and an emotional or psychological perspective.

If you win, great. If you lose, ask the client where you went astray and hope that you get a truthful response. My experience of responding to formal or advertised briefs is that they require a lot of time, effort and expense, with about a one or two in ten chance of success. Other consultants I know have a better strike rate, but they won't tell me their secret. Clients usually do not give consultants much time to prepare and lodge a proposal, but often take a much longer time to make a decision. This apparent misallocation of time is frustrating to consultants who want to prepare a quality proposal and find out quickly whether they have won or lost. On a number of occasions, I have not been formally notified of the result and have had to ask for the answer. It is not unusual, either, to be informed that no one has obtained the job, and that the decision has been made not to go ahead with the project.

If the project is won, then the real work starts—but it is no hardship, because you will now be getting paid for the effort.

As a general rule, it is a good idea to follow the credo: *Underpromise and overdeliver.*

PROJECT INITIATION—CLIENT'S POINT OF VIEW

From an enterprise perspective, projects typically go through a specific set of stages, again more iterative than sequential. These comprise the preliminary and preparatory stages, tender request and consultant selection, and project planning.

Preliminary stage

During the preliminary stage, needs are determined and justified, feasibility is determined along with the risks involved, and initial budgets are developed. This is normally done by managers themselves, but sometimes consultants can be used to assist.

It is important that the end users of the project outcomes are involved in at least this stage.

Preparatory stage

During the preparatory stage, specific requirements/expectations are set, firm budgets are confirmed, and the project time, task, location facilities and internal staffing elements are outlined.

This activity can result in the project being undertaken internally, or the decision can be taken to tender or contract it out.

Tender request and consultant selection

If the decision is to tender out, an RFP is prepared and the organization informs consultants—whether by direct request or advertisement—that it is now a potential client.

If the proposed project activities are new to the client or the need has only been loosely thought through, then the selection stage can be difficult for the enterprise to navigate, because those concerned are 'working in the dark'. This is often reflected in an RFP that is confusing and seemingly illogical in its timing and budget allowance. Consultants responding to these types of RFP must be careful to make the potential client aware of the possible implications of such perceived anomalies, while at the same time not disadvantaging their submission.

Project planning

When a consultant has been selected, the next stage of project planning is extremely important. As Eisenhower said, 'Plans are nothing. Planning is everything'. Although the client has developed an RFP and the consultant has submitted a successful proposal that will be the basis of the project action, it is still necessary for both parties to develop jointly an agreed plan for the project. The consultant and client must work as a team if the project is to be successful. This plan should give mutual clarity to expectations, tasks, resources, schedules, budgets, contingencies, control/reporting requirements and staffing responsibilities.

It is from this point on that the consultant is actively engaged in the consulting cycle described in chapter 6.

PROJECT MANAGEMENT DURING THE CONSULTING CYCLE

Partnering with clients

Anecdotal and some research evidence suggests that clients are not always happy with consultant services. Sometimes this dissatisfaction has more to do with failings on the client side, but assignments may also fail because of differing views about the problem, differing expectations about the outcome/deliverables or relationship/trust problems.

Consultants often run into trouble when they tell a client things that the client does not want to hear (which may lead to the client 'killing the messenger with bad news') or give the client solutions that are unexpected or organizationally unacceptable. Consultants must always be aware that they have to offer what is possible and not necessarily the ideal.

It is important, then, that the client take a key role in helping to prevent dissatisfaction with a consultant's performance. Clients should establish clear outcome expectations, define roles in the project, be flexible when necessary and support the consultant so that internal credibility is established. If a client is not taking this key role, then astute consultants who value their reputation must help them in the establishment and agreement of project parameters.

It needs to be recognized, however, that a process consulting approach, or a project involving rather more intangible outcomes like culture change or improved morale or communication, will not be able to be planned as systematically as suggested here.

There must be a nominated person from the consulting side who is the designated project leader and also a client representative (a 'counterpart') who is responsible for the client's interests.

It is becoming common these days to find that organizations have appointed internal consultants, who are often the counterparts for external consultants. While these people may not be called 'internal consultant', they will usually be in areas such as human resources management, policy and planning, and corporate communication, the typical staff functions that provide services to line functions. It is the changing nature of staff functions that has moved them into consulting roles rather than advisory and performance roles.

Internal consultants are in a strong position to help external consultants make a difference to organizational performance, because they are 'in' the organization. They know it intimately and yet can be objective about line activities, and will remain with the organization to follow up implementation activities after the external consultant has exited.

They can act as 'boundary riders' and as a conduit for new ideas from external sources. Because they usually do not have any line authority, they have to operate in persuasive mode to influence organizational performance, and in this sense have a similar job to do, with the same tools, as external consultants.

Implementation

Consulting projects may involve solving problems, improving systems, procedures and performance, defining organizational structures or any other activity that is aimed at satisfying client needs. The implementation stage is where consulting cycle activities are matched with the project plan.

The main elements of managing an implementation project are as follows:

- *Development of a work plan:* If you are doing this as a consultant, it entails putting much more detail into the plan developed for presentation to the client to convince him or her—or them—that your joint solution is sound.

The work plan, which may include Gantt charts and program evaluation review technique (PERT) programs, represents the what, when, who and how much of the project, and should identify the skill levels required. The whole plan must be discussed and agreed with everyone concerned prior to its implementation.

It is a good idea to attempt to predict any problems that may interrupt progress and to include plans for contingent action should these occur.

- *Establishment of controls over the implementation activities:* To ensure that the project is going to schedule and within budget and is producing a quality result, indicators of time, cost and resource use must be built into the plan.

  A project committee can be established to monitor progress, or an independent reviewer/s can be given the monitoring task.

- *Selection and training of personnel needed to undertake the project:* This phase is crucial to the project's success. The consultant and client need to work on this, with selected staff having a clear idea of their duties and responsibilities in relation to the consultant. People may already be available as part of the system being changed, or they may need to be recruited from outside that system or even outside the enterprise.

  The size and complexity of most implementation projects mean that the project manager will have to delegate many tasks to the selected project personnel. As with most management positions, such delegation must not become abdication, which can give a false impression of democratic management.

- *Installation of needed physical facilities:* This requires planning before the installation phase and could mean considerable negotiation and agreement on any changes to existing facilities, equipment or working conditions.

- *Development of standards and documentation:* These will become the normal operational mechanics when the change is made. Most new systems need some form of standard setting and documentation development so that the solution being implemented can be 'institutionalized'.

Changes to the plan are made as required through consultation with the client. Project activities can be handed over progressively to regular client staff if the activities are to become part of the organization's routine operation.

Presentations

Current trends indicate that presentations, as well as being useful at proposal and final report stages, are also common during projects, and in some cases the presentation package is replacing the lengthy report (the 'dust gatherer') as the key deliverable if implementation is not part of the assignment.

Strong presentations are crucial for successful consulting project management, and delivering a top service depends on an ability to express ideas orally, in both formal and informal situations. Chapter 6 provides some advice on how to do this (see p. 70). Consultants, typically being technically and analytically inclined, often find presentations difficult and uncomfortable, but they are part of the job and serve the consulting project cycle in two ways: as a tool to support the consulting process and as a deliverable to the client. The major benefits are that they provide an opportunity for the consultant to adjust findings and analysis on the basis of client feedback; they build credibility, trust and rapport; and they give some emotional and personal dynamism to what can be a dry and uninspiring report in written form.

The objective of a presentation is to create an exchange of ideas between the presenter and the audience that builds shared understanding, agreement and action. The goal is not to impress but to involve the client.

Monitoring

While the final project plan is the key mechanism for controlling the project, a consultant cannot escape from the requirement to keep track of the project. This is done by recording copious notes of what he or she has done, what interim results have been achieved, what problems have been encountered and what changes have been made to the original plan.

At any stage of the project, you need to be able to answer client questions such as 'When will you complete this task?', 'What is the project status?', 'What problems have you encountered to date?', 'Why is the production department complaining that this project is taking too much of their time?', 'Why did you not inform me that you did not interview the Sales Manager as you planned to do?'.

There is thus the need for many of the project management tools that are mentioned elsewhere: the project plan itself (and associated aids such as Gantt charts or computer-based programs like critical path method or PERT for task/time/resources scheduling), time and expense reports, internal status reports and client accounts and billing.

In addition, the project working papers, which provide the historical substantiation of work performed, are necessary documents, as they form the basis for draft and final recommendations and reports.

Evaluation

At the conclusion of the project, the outcomes are evaluated. It is useful for consultant and client to sit down together and look at all aspects of the project in terms of its successful (or otherwise) conduct and results. Such an audit is of value to both parties for their future decision-making on project activities—whether carried out jointly again or separately.

The final act

The consultant exits gracefully, leaving—he or she hopes—a satisfied client behind.

8 | Learning to do the job

The new consultant will come to the job with a certain amount of work experience, always in one or more functional areas and perhaps also at a management level.

It is beyond my intentions to delve into learning at the functional level here, and I will say little about organizational and management, and interpersonal skills. My main concern is how one learns about marketing and about consulting as a technical process.

ORGANIZATIONAL AND MANAGEMENT SKILLS

Organizational and management skills can be learned by experience, if one is perceptive enough to interpret experience into a framework that can be used to deal with organization and management systems in a constructive manner.

It also helps to study some of the large amount of literature on the topic, either informally by private study or more formally through short or long educational courses offered by a variety of institutions.

In Australia, Technical and Further Education courses, Australian Institute of Management courses, university undergraduate and postgraduate programs, and in-company courses in organizations and management are some of the ways in which consultants, or intending consultants, can become familiar with the relevant topic areas. Similar institutions exist in other countries.

Since the late 1800s, various schools of thought in regard to organizations and management have prevailed, and the importance of scientific management, classical management, the behavioural school, the quantitative school, and contingency and systems theory to consultancy needs to be recognized. A particularly good summary of these schools and theories is given by John Ivancevich et al. (1997).

INTERPERSONAL SKILLS

Interpersonal skills, other than inherent qualities, can also be learned through experience, as well as through development programs. Learning to be more effective in relations with people is the subject of countless personal development programs, so consultants are never short of opportunities to be exposed to the various methods advocated—at a price, of course.

Communication is a good example of an interpersonal area in which there are plenty of 'how to' suggestions for various settings. Some are included in this book (see chapters 3 and 5).

MARKETING AND CONSULTING TECHNICAL SKILLS

The acquisition of marketing skill involves learning how best to sell your services to an often doubting market. I will leave discussion of this topic until chapter 9 (see p. 119), where it is covered in the context of the requirements for running a practice.

Consulting technical skills comprise consulting cycle, process consulting and project management skills. Chapters 6 and 7 discuss what these skills entail and how they are applied. This section is devoted to how they can be learned.

While managers who enter the profession will have a good idea of how to manage functions, people and projects in general, they will have little or no idea (apart from hearsay) of the consulting cycle or process consulting or marketing their service.

The basic learning and development options include guided self-learning, mentoring, education programs, and on-the-job training.

Self-learning

The most immediate way to learn about these matters is self-learning—that is, by finding a book or two on consulting and reading them.

I hope that *Mind for Hire* is of help to someone entering the profession, and there are plenty of others that deal with the total consulting area or specific parts of that whole. Appendix B and the reference list at the end of this book indicate the extent of the literature available in both book and article form.

Mentoring

Contact and discussions with an experienced consultant who is prepared to share the results of that experience and to mentor and guide you through the early phases of learning to do the job can also be of great value to the newcomer. Because of the range of consultancy areas and the skill disparities between consultants, the choice of mentor is crucial.

A mentor should be experienced in the area in which you intend to work, and should be professionally credible. The best indicator of professional recognition is membership of the IMC, with a CMC qualification.

Education programs

Education programs are not as readily available as books and mentors, but there have been efforts made in recent years to provide such learning opportunities.

In 1998, the IMC in Australia introduced its Professional Development (PD) Program, which was produced under the auspices of the National PD Committee. Three modules form the present program, but these could be modified and more added over coming years:

- Marketing Management Consulting Services;
- Delivering Quality Outcomes;
- Practice Management.

Each module package contains a presenter's guide, a session plan, copies of overhead slides and a participant manual. The program is designed in this manner in order for each State chapter to be able to run modules as required as a precursor to members taking the CMC examination.

The IMC Federal Executive is also in the process of negotiating articulation of these modules into Graduate Certificate, Graduate Diploma and Masters level programs in a number of universities.

The modules are an important element of the IMC PD strategy, which aims to:

- motivate all IMC members to invest in their continuing professional development;
- equip IMC members with the knowledge and skills required to operate professionally in a complex, changing and challenging marketplace;
- focus on CMC by providing as many IMC members as possible with the opportunity to achieve CMC status;
- provide IMC members, their colleagues and clients with an advanced forum through which to learn, influence and network.

The IMC's PD strategy focuses on working at five levels:

- State Chapter sponsored activities: forums, networking, master classes, luncheons, etc.;
- IMC PD modules/tertiary courses (as described above);
- CMC: training, pre-examination workshops, CMC collegial forums;
- IMC national conference planned on an annual basis;
- ICMCI Asia Pacific conferences: these are held every two years in a different country in the region.

ICMCI is the global body that provides a linking and liaison mechanism for over thirty country member institutes. The CMC badge is recognized by all member institutes, and this portability makes the CMC a useful qualification for consultants moving or working internationally. The IMC in Australia was a founding member of this umbrella organization and is also a key member of the Asia Pacific group.

Universities in Australia do not usually offer units in management consulting. Two exceptions are the Graduate School of Management at The University of Western Australia, which introduced an elective unit called Management and Consulting into its Master of Business Administration (MBA) program in 1996, and Royal Melbourne Institute of Technology University, which offers a unit called Consulting and Networking for Managers in its Advanced Diploma in Management.

On-the-job training

Big firms versus small firms

A favourite route for people wanting to get into consulting is to complete an MBA and apply to one or other of the big consulting firms such as Boston Consulting, Ernst & Young, PriceWaterhouse Coopers, the PA Consulting Group or Andersen Consulting. Most of these big firms cite an MBA as a 'must have' qualification for selection.

An alternative is to join a small firm, either formally as an employee or more informally as a subcontractor. Another way is to start on your own as a sole operator or in partnership with a like-minded colleague.

It is becoming more prevalent in the current climate of downsizing to find a number of ex–private enterprise and ex–public sector managers putting up a consulting shingle. Some of them are contracted back to their erstwhile organizations for special project work, but many have to start from scratch in attracting clients.

One of the most critical processes at work in consulting firms of whatever size is the growth and development of the firm's people. Even the loner or the partners in a joint operation must not neglect the need to keep up to date with issues, trends and methods relevant to their sphere of consulting activity.

Different stages of growth, different sizes of firm and the different education and experience of consultants often dictate the need and type of development program/s required. A big established firm may use orientation training, on-the-job training, mentoring, self-directed learning and external education as development processes to cater for all its staff development needs. A small firm just starting will have limited time and resources for consultant development, even though it may well be required if the principal/s are new to the consulting task. A recent graduate will have different development needs to a professional consultant with many years' experience.

A major issue that arises when clients use the so-called 'big six' firms is that of 'Who is the consultant?'.

The reputation of a big firm is generated over a long period of time, and services are often sold by the senior and most well known partners and consultants. This means that relatively inexperienced consultants can be the ones actually doing the fieldwork. In these circumstances, the client–consultant relationship and the operation of the assignment are more complex and much harder to manage.

Some cynics talk of big firm staff as 'finders', 'minders' and 'grinders'. Top people find the work, middle-level people manage or mind the work, and grinders do the work.

One of the benefits for newer and more junior consultants in a big firm is that they can use the experience and contacts gained to go out and start their own practice—a common means of start-up that gets around the problems of attracting new clients (discussed further in chapter 9). Obviously, this is not to the advantage of the big consulting firms that have trained them!

International consulting

If the firm is aiming at an international profile, it must ensure that its consultants have the cultural knowledge and adaptability needed to work in this difficult market. Consultants are familiar with the fact that every organization has a unique culture that determines how things are done and what behaviour is acceptable, but working internationally adds another dimension to the cultural factor.

Consultants practising (or wishing to practise) internationally need to be alert to the necessity of adapting their general consulting approach to the specific needs of situations where they are faced with political, economic, legal, social and cultural conditions often quite different to those with which they are familiar.

These conditions, particularly cultural conditions, result in business practices that are also different, and consultants must be aware that their knowledge and experience of home country business practice will likely be largely irrelevant in the new context.

The business practice outcomes of profitability, cost containment, quality, quantity and job satisfaction are more or less universal requirements, but their priority and weighting and the methods of achieving them are different from business to business and from country to country. Thus the issue becomes not 'what' we do but 'why, how, when and where' we do it and 'who' does it.

The Western approach that I advocate in this book is not necessarily applicable in Asia, for example, where logic and reason often have to take second place to intuition, emotion and cultural factors such as family loyalty, hierarchical operation and connections.

Working as an expatriate consultant requires much more sensitivity, flexibility and tolerance than are needed at home.

Skills development

Although programs tend to be unique to each firm, they all try to develop skills and knowledge and appropriate attitudes in the following areas:

- the generic consulting skills of marketing and selling, organizational and change analysis, creativity, data gathering, problem-solving, communication, team building, and influencing and negotiating;
- the technical skill upgrading needed to keep abreast of new techniques/ideas;
- the practice itself—specific knowledge necessary to work with the firm's procedures and methodologies.

A consultant must be able to assess the client's needs, restate them in a clear, concise, impartial and complete manner, and put forth a plan to address them. The thinking process involved should be open, flexible, analytical and creative.

Creativity and pattern recognition are two skills that typically take a back seat as people grow older and more conservative, set in their ways and 'I have the answer' prone, and so a good development program will concentrate on these areas. However, this can be an ambitious expectation, considering that the teachers themselves probably have been schooled and have gained their experience in the analytical and quantitative methodology that is favoured by Western education.

9 | Running the business

The majority of consultants in Australia are sole operators or partners or employees in what is essentially a small business. Therefore, I have no hesitation in stating bluntly that a consultant must know how to run a small business. How the business is to be structured and financed, how to manage cash flows, how to market the business, how to grow the business and how to set up the reward and tax regime for the business are just a few key decision areas in which a wrong decision or two can spell disaster. The failure rate of small business in Australia is reckoned to be as high as 60 per cent within the first two years of operation, and so anyone starting a small business of any type has to aim at being in the 40 per cent that do survive.

Consultants are often worse off than other small business operators. Although they, in common with other new business owner/operators, are unfamiliar with the principles of small business management, they are often also unfamiliar with the consulting cycle and its application, despite having knowledge of the functional area in which they wish to consult.

This chapter does not present a fulsome description of how to run a small business, but covers some points that are particularly relevant to consulting businesses. For many new consultants starting outside the big firms, a course in small business management would not go astray—and perhaps this should be added to the list of required skills (chapter 3) and the skills to be learned (chapter 8).

The points covered here are in the areas of business planning, finance, administration and that vital aspect of business operation — marketing.

BUSINESS PLANNING

The need for a business plan

There are arguments for and against business planning — most arising from the debate about the uncertainty and unpredictability of the future. However, with a business plan in place, a consultant can make an educated choice as to whether or not, and how, to deviate from the plan.

The process of going through a planning exercise can be as beneficial as producing the plan. Because it is an iterative process, there are opportunities to question, change and rethink the results.

Elements of a business plan

The plan for a consultancy should consider such strategic issues as the mission/goal for the business, and whether or not to grow the practice, to extend a service to a wider market or to expand the services performed by current staff. In a few pages, it is useful to have:

- a description of the current practice (or the new one) and its market, services, structure, staffing, and strengths and weaknesses. A major first decision for a new consulting practice is its name. Most starters use their name and become 'Bill Brown and Associates'. However, catchier identifiers should perhaps be considered. I called my initial human resources management consultancy Industrial Personnel and Training Services but soon changed it to Intrain, which I thought was easier to remember and to place into logo form;
- a list of factors or needs that will cause change in the future;
- a list of changes that should be made to the business when these changes occur;

- a forecast of revenue/profit expected;
- a list of risks anticipated and the tactical steps required to manage them.

At a more detailed and shorter term level, the plan should include a financial plan, a marketing plan, and a staff selection and development plan if relevant.

Types of business plan

Depending on the stage of development of the business and the strategy chosen, a business plan can be a 'start-up' plan, a 'business-as-usual' plan or a 'business growth' plan.

Start-up plan

An important consideration at any development stage is whether the market wants to buy what you want to sell. You might think that clients need or want what you have to offer. But do they? If they don't, it will be hard to sell services to them.

The start-up plan is very much a predictions-based plan and has to be detailed and convincing if it is to be used to obtain finance. In essence, it should describe the what, why, how, when, where, who and how much in regard to start-up.

Business-as-usual plan

The business-as-usual plan is a base business plan that continues current staffing levels, traditional utilization and current trends in cost and expense structure. The purpose is to establish the revenue and profit that can be generated by maintaining the current business assumptions.

Business growth plan

The business growth plan describes how the business will look and what its cost, expense and profit situation will be given that market growth expectations are met. It accommodates significant staffing and revenue growth.

FINANCE PLANNING

Key early decisions in any consulting business planning are related to the factors that mainly determine the financial and cash flow profile of the business. These factors are billing (charge-out) rates, expected consultant utilization rates (billable time), consultant salaries and contractor fees, and expected overheads and other expenses.

Setting and assessing rates and fees

To set charge-out rates and billable time, the important assumptions are those made in relation to expected hours to be spent on behalf of clients, the proportion of those hours that will produce billable results, and the rate to be charged in order to produce a viable income stream.

The following simple example indicates the assumptions that a sole operator could make in order to forecast a gross income of $84,000 per year:

> Available hours per year: 2,000
> Hours spent on behalf of clients: 1,200
> Billable time—70 per cent of hours spent: 840 hours
> Rate = $100 per hour—therefore, income = $84,000
> (Note that the yearly earning rate is about $40 per hour and the actual client hours earning rate is about $70 per hour)

Most project fees also include an expenses item to cover travel, parking, report preparation and other incidentals.

The difference between elapsed time and consulting time is important to consider in any project equation. The project may well take place over a period of three months (elapsed time), but the consulting time allocated to that project could be one and a half months. It should be clear in the submission how much consulting time is being allocated over what elapsed time period, in order to pre-empt possible confusion later in the project.

Itemizing the amount of time spent by each consultant can also keep you from falling into the 'fee trap'. You may, for example, quote a fee of $24,000 for the six-week (30 days/240 hours) job above, based on a charge-out rate of $100/hour. This will be fine if one consultant is used, but if two are used for the period, then your actual charge-out rate is $50/hour and you will not have much left over after paying the consultants and covering your overheads. The result of the 'fee trap' can be just as upsetting as spending more time on a job than estimated without being able to raise the fee.

While on this topic, a helpful hint is: never apologize for your price. Clients have a tendency to multiply your daily rate by 360 to calculate your 'dramatic annual earnings', but ignore the fact that you do not get 100 per cent consulting time in any elapsed time period and that operating expenses must be considered.

How much should a client be willing to pay for a consultant? As a rule of thumb, Azimuth Consulting Limited, an international consulting firm with its head office in Wellington, New Zealand, suggests that clients should:

- take the annual salary of the employee (or add up the annual salaries of the employees) who could perform the assignment;
- multiply this by the number of months it would take and divide by twelve;
- multiply this figure by 1.5, the usual costs of benefits for an employee;
- take this figure and multiply by 1.6, a reasonable markup for the consultant.

For example, if a project required one person of a usual salary of $100,000 for six months, the calculations would be:

$100,000 x 6/12 = $50,000
$50,000 x 1.5 = $75,000
$75,000 x 1.6 = $120,000
(This is an overall multiplier of 2.4)

Assume twenty working days per month for the consultant for six months, or 120 days. If the consultant charges $1,000 per day for this assignment, plus or minus 20 per cent, the fees are within a reasonable range for the skill level involved.

After such a calculation, clients must assess whether the fee is reasonable and feasible for the consultant. Reasonable means whether what the consultant is being asked to do for the time and money involved is fair to the consultant. For example, asking a consultant to lead the turnaround of a company and expecting it to be done in three months is unreasonable, even if the client offers $250,000. It just can't be done in that time, no matter how good and experienced the consultant is. A company turnaround takes at least six months and more likely a year or more to do.

Feasible means that given the client circumstances, the results expected are reasonable and the client is willing to hire the consultant and has the money to pay.

Some international aid agencies will accept fee quotes as realistic from consulting company providers if they use a consultant home salary multiplier of about 2.5 to 3.0 to determine the charge-out rate for an international consulting fee allocation.

Overheads

Typical *direct costs* are salaries, benefits, commissions/bonuses, non-recoverable travel, education/conferences and recruiting. Typical *indirect costs* are those associated with marketing, administration, office services and facilities.

A useful rule of thumb for service businesses is to calculate that about 50 per cent of income will be absorbed by operating expenses, thus leaving 50 per cent as a reward for actually performing the service.

In the previous example (p. 114), using this rule the consultant could expect to receive only $42,000 in-pocket income for the year, which would perhaps increase once the business's net income and tax payments had been calculated. For consultants able to run their business from home 'on the smell of an oilrag', the in-pocket return is higher, but some percentage will be swallowed up by overheads.

The fact that a percentage of your charge-out rate will be needed to cover overheads should be a consideration when setting rates.

A problem that used to catch the starting consultant unawares was the need to allow for provisional tax, which was charged on the basis of the first year of operation. This made a large hole in cash flow and had an adverse effect on the whole operation if funds were not set aside to cover it. The introduction of pay-as-you-go tax, which replaces provisional tax, means that cash flow implications must be recognized and allowed for, particularly if returns are lodged quarterly.

Consultants lacking expertise in accounting would be well advised to acquire advice and assistance before starting operations.

Other charging methods

Other methods of charging include a flat project fee, day rate plus expenses, and fixed rate plus expenses.

Often a client has a fixed budget for a job, and you have to decide whether you can do the job for that fee and still make a profit. Circumstances and your need for cash flow will determine your decision in these situations.

The basic difference between a fixed price and a day rate is that the consultant takes the risk with the former, and the client takes the risk with the latter—the risk being that the estimate (either the consultant's or the client's) of the size of the project is wrong. However a deal is struck, there is always a conscious or unconscious application of an hourly rate that represents your sense of your value as a contribution to the client organization.

The hourly rate can be a slippery figure and its realism can depend on how well you estimate the hours it will take to complete a project. For example, if you estimate that a job will take 100 hours and your charge-out rate is $100 per hour, your consulting fee to the client will be $10,000. If the job actually takes 125 hours, you are really working for only $80 per hour. Many consultants do not like to calculate the actual hours on a job because it deflates their ego and puts their estimating skills in a poor light. However, practicality suggests that work is better than no work, and income is better than no income, and so they are prepared to swallow the pill and accept the discrepancy between effort and reward (see comments in the IMC benchmark survey in chapter 4).

I write these words with feeling because I know from experience that on most projects, I spend more time than has been budgeted because I want a quality outcome rather than an outcome where the hours estimated match those used.

In the current economic climate, consultants are increasingly finding themselves faced with limited client budgets and are almost obliged to become price takers rather than price makers in order to remain competitive.

Ultimately, what is really important in regard to finances is not the fee level or the overhead proportion or profits, but how much you end up with after the taxation department has finished working you over!

The idea of a success fee has never really taken off in the consulting arena. This is because consulting solutions that pay dividends in the short term might prove costly in the long term, and because of the fact that the client plays such an important role in whether a successful outcome is achieved or not.

Payment on results is considered to be a 'discreditable act' by the IMC, which claims that the nature of consulting determines that a fee for a specified service is the most appropriate means of payment. Other factors leading to this stand include the difficulty of identifying and measuring real results achieved by an intervention, and the distinct possibility that the client's and the consultant's assessment of results could be in conflict.

Budgeting

Planning in a small firm with one or two consultants need not be as sophisticated as suggested above, but it helps at least to make a forecast of income and expenses, probably by quarter.

There is evidence to suggest that decision-making in small business is more reactive than innovative and more subjective than analytical, but that does not mean that you have to follow the norm. Being innovative and analytical could put you ahead of the competition.

ADMINISTRATION

Other administrative decisions to be made early in a start-up situation relate to:

- premises from which to operate;
- equipment such as phones and computers to purchase or lease;
- establishment of a working relationship with an accountant (as I suggested earlier, if you are not one yourself);
- setting up basic accounting and office forms and procedures;
- arranging workers' compensation (if you set up a company) and professional indemnity insurance.

The points made in chapter 7 on project management are relevant here—particularly what I call the 'tracer documentation' such as the project plan, time sheets, invoices and working notes that chart and monitor the operational activities.

I find that it helps during the progress of a consultancy for me to keep in mind the client's point of view. I have been chosen by the client because he or she believes that my work will be of high quality, that I will have a comfortable personality fit and I will deliver what is required on time, at a competitive price.

Matching my skills with that set of expectations requires considerable effort, and the ability to be flexible when needed to adjust the project plan to the changing needs and circumstances of the client, and to amend my administrative procedures accordingly.

MARKETING

Other than the activities involved in the consulting cycle itself (chapter 6), the most important operational aspect of consulting is the activity of marketing. Without clients you have no consultancy.

Sources of new business

In regard to marketing, research shows that most new business flows through present client activities, referral relationships, community visibility activities and potential client targeting activities (Keeble, Bryson and Wood 1994).

Present clients

With present clients, the purpose of business development should be directed towards:

- retention;
- expansion of services through cross-marketing;
- generation of referral business.

All three can be approached in a systematic manner through maintaining a quality service, developing personal relationships of trust, and gaining a thorough knowledge of the client, client staff and the client organization and its problems/opportunities.

Referrals

Referral relationships (networking) can begin from current clients but can be developed through third parties like other professionals or organizations. The strategy for building relationships should be focused on establishing personal contact, and this can be done through seminar attendance, professional publications and attendance at social functions.

Community visibility activities

Community visibility can be gained through advertising, newsletters, seminars and workshops, speeches, publications, press relations, trade shows and participation in professional or community organizations.

Potential client targeting activities

Potential client targeting requires market analysis in light of your service skills, followed by some method of establishing contact with chosen targets. In marketing terms, it is necessary to cover the four P's—product, price, place and promotion.

Many of the decisions related to these should be covered in the business plan, but it is also useful to consider them specifically in the context of a marketing approach. Probably the most important P is product—that is, your service. As part of your initial planning, it is imperative that you decide exactly what your service and your market are. Will you try to be all things to all people, or will you select one or two specific functional areas to aim at? Will you consult to all levels of management, or will you concentrate on the top level only?

If you cannot explain clearly who you are, what you do and what benefits you can provide, then you will find it difficult to promote your service at any price in any place. A colleague of mine, marketing researcher and presenter Barry Urquhart, suggests that you do not have to be better; you have to be different. The importance of determining your niche in terms of product and positioning cannot be overemphasized.

Elements of the marketing strategy

Thomas Greenbaum (1990) has developed a special consulting marketing mix that contains nine P's: planning, product, positioning, professionalism, people, price, place, promotion and packaging. His additional P's can be described in the following terms:

- *Planning* consists of setting the direction for the business—services, target market, finances, structure and staffing.
- *Positioning* establishes how you want your business to be viewed by the client/prospect population—the personality and character of your business.
- *Professionalism* relates to quality, ethics and community professional activities.
- *People* refers to the types of clientele you are trying to attract and the quality of personnel in the practice.
- *Packaging* refers to the look of the practice—the graphics of the stationery, business cards and brochures and the decor of the offices.

It is a useful mix because it brings into focus some other important elements that form the foundation of a sound marketing strategy.

The quality of marketing is more important than the quantity, and plenty of thought should go into the promotional material used and the methods chosen to promote the business to new clients. Promotional material like brochures, business cards and letterheads should be attractive, distinctive, readable, honest and clear, without being flashy and pompous.

Marketing, as has been noted earlier, is usually not a strength for management consultants, myself included, who are more comfortable doing the job than generating jobs. If you are a 'rainmaker', as good marketers are sometimes called, then you are indeed fortunate. If you are not, then you have to learn some of the skills involved, or employ someone who has them or outsource the job to an agency or person who can do it on your behalf.

10 Learning from experience

One thing I have learned is the value of an experienced and insightful mentor. This is valuable to anyone in any sphere of life, of course, and I have been lucky with my mentors in both management and consulting. In my book on management (Smith 1994), I use ideas and practices gained over many years of working with talented people in the human resource, general management and consulting areas.

One, in particular—Geoffrey Hutton (1972b)—has the advantage of being a good consultant as well as academic, and his fields of psychology and psychoanalysis are a solid foundation for understanding the often subtle though powerful behavioural forces at play between people in organizations.

One of his legacies is a set of research and consulting aphorisms or proverbs for practice (Hutton 1979), which he distributed to his students and which I will share with readers because I consider them to be useful insights into the consulting process and its application. He did not think it possible to conduct consulting practice on the basis of picking up a few rules of thumb as represented by these aphorisms (exaggerations to highlight a point of view) and was aware of the paradox entailed in proposing them. The best way of learning is from one's own experience, and so he offered his aphorisms as companions to experience and guides to conceptual understanding, not as a set of golden rules.

Following these aphorisms are some further understandings I have learned from my own experience.

HUTTON'S RESEARCH AND CONSULTING APHORISMS

The accompanying written material to each of Hutton's aphorisms is quite substantial, and only a brief note of explanation for each is given here.

The problem is never about what it seems to be about

I used a form of this aphorism as a maxim in my management book (Smith 1994) and discuss a version of it in chapter 6 when considering the difference between symptoms and deeper problems. Commonly, management conceives problems as being about methods or techniques when they are often problems of control or of creativity. Problems conceived in terms of 'communication' or 'team building' may be problems of conflicting objectives, co-operation and trust. Problems of 'getting commitment' may turn out to be difficulties in 'getting my subordinates to do what I want'. The consultant must interpret the meaning of the presented symptom.

Completion will take three times as long as the last estimate

Here the point is that change usually takes much longer to achieve and institutionalize than managers and consultants generally expect or hope. There is a tendency to think that the first serious work on a problem has been done by the consultant because it is new to him or her. However, there will always be a history of attempts to investigate and deal with the problem and a history of preparation and preamble to calling in consultants. There is also, on the part of those who commission consultants, a tendency to expect quick results once they have made up their minds.

While it may not take a consultant a long time to 'rumble' the situation, actually getting a result accepted and implemented is a different issue altogether.

If things seem to be going well, beware, because there will be resisting forces somewhere that will produce delay.

There is always a muddle in the middle

No project is going to be as clear cut as suggested by the proposal. One's conceptions will change and much rethinking will occur. Information, in other words, affects our ideas. Nothing in consulting is neat and tidy and, as an investigation proceeds, things can get very murky indeed. In these circumstances, one has to focus on the end result of improved performance and sort out the muddle as quickly as possible in these terms, whatever the original terms of reference (within reason, of course).

The most important item of equipment is the wastepaper basket

The art of managing a consulting project involves judging when to:

- change direction to what appears to be a more fruitful line to the client;
- recognize that you have enough information to identify the problem;
- recognize serendipitous discoveries or felicitous chances;
- drop your favoured design in preference for the more operational design suggested by the client.

The point is not to stick slavishly to the proposal when it needs modification, and also not to be led down tributaries that are not going to help the project. Consultants should be explicit about their own wastepaper basket rejections and tolerant towards other people's choices.

The right to practise is earned

This question of legitimacy is of vital importance to consultants. The assumption that 'because I can practise, I have a right to' needs to be questioned. More reliance should be placed on the assumption that, whatever one's competence or expertise, and whatever one's practice, if one's concern is to be consulted or to have notice taken of one's 'expert' advice or to try to help, then one should *earn the right and expect to have to earn the right continuously.*

You earn the right by doing what you claim to be able to do, by displaying understanding and knowledge, by getting on with clients and being authentic and trustworthy. Clients test out these things using a number of manipulative techniques, and your toleration of these manipulations will involve you in a determination to show that you can earn the right and that you will not be tricked, sidetracked or forced out of role.

It involves a capacity to wait, to respond to initiatives, to start where the client is, and to build up a case record of being helpful and successfully accomplishing a number of small finite, intermediate jobs.

Because consulting involves a relationship between two systems (client system and consultant system), consultants should not forget the guardian angels and the gatekeepers in organizational interventions. In particular, the consultant must try to ensure that powerful cover and support from the top is forthcoming, because it is essential to the success of any change effort.

Question the assumptions

This is a plea to make clear where you stand in relation to the purposes and values of the enterprise with which you are working.

The contrasting views that a consultant should either accept and not question the purposes and values of client systems or act as a moral advocate of a particular set of personal purposes and values are rejected. A different view sees the importance of seeking, early in a project, agreement on the purpose of the project and of making explicit the values and beliefs that surround and control the work—to determine 'what is' without prejudice and without value judgment or statements of 'what ought to be'.

This means that a consultant should not become trapped in the client system, should not let things pass without question if they need questioning (even if it takes courage to flag certain issues) and should not allow him/herself to be manipulated by the client.

The story of the Emperor's new clothes (by Hans Christian Andersen) illustrates the meaning of this aphorism. A key point for consultants to remember about this story is that the Emperor, despite being made aware of his nakedness, continues to parade naked because he does not want to admit his foolishness and lose face!

When considering approved written policy, it is unwise to assume that the policy is actually implemented. Approval does not always mean that an organization's written policy will be followed. Wise consultants check that action matches the words.

Work where the problem is

This is a broader maxim than starting where the client is—a familiar call for most consultants, even if it is often more honoured in the breach, particularly by experts.

The crux of this matter is:

- the ownership of the problem;
- the discretion to act.

As Reg Revans (1982) has said: who knows? Who cares? Who can?

Time and again, we find the attribution of a problem to somebody else, without regard to the effect of the problem on the complainant, and without regard to the contribution he or she is making to it. Time and again, we find the declaration that the trouble or the appropriate point of remedial action lies somewhere else—'It's the system'—without consideration of what the complainant can do about it him/herself.

What to do if your apparent client refuses to consider his/her position, refuses to explore, insists that action lies elsewhere, insists on assistance to do something that is clearly outside his/her discretion, or is seeking help beyond your competence or attempting to solve what you firmly regard, with reason, to be unsolvable? The answer is simple to see but may be too costly to do, though it must be done: *if it's a non-starter, don't start.*

Feelings are useful

Process consulting, as opposed to specialist advice or technical assistance, is dependent on dialogue between consultant and client, and hence the consultant's feelings take on a key role in these projects where the consultant gets close to the client's own involvement.

When you are investigating, or attempting to help, people in social situations, one of the best indicators of what is going on is the effect that the people or the situation is having on you. Consultants should not ignore themselves as measuring devices.

A corollary is that consultants must understand their feelings and also realize that, try as they might, it is impossible to be completely objective in any consultancy. First impressions and the hints a consultant picks up may well be acute indicators of the main politics in a situation. It is a great pity if they are not recognized and recorded in field notes.

Every structure tells a story

This aphorism was originally stated by Cyril Sofer (1961).

Not all consulting is just about feelings, and there is a need to come to terms with understanding structures and systems. The structure that appears or that is extant at the moment is very likely there for reasons of internal or external political history, which may have a good deal to do with accommodating the interests of powerful people or powerful groups.

In a sense, you can treat the structure observed not as a logically derived instrument for getting the work done—what it may or may not be—but as a historical trace of past events.

Procedures themselves can be presented as logical solutions to problems of work and control, although they are also likely to be used as scapegoats by other people—for example, 'We can't do anything with that budget control system in the way'.

As well as the official system, the organization has an unofficial work system and structure that have a major impact on how work is carried out. The importance of the unofficial system to the operation of the official system is well illustrated when a union works to rule (official procedure) and the organization grinds to a halt. Whatever the system, there will be feelings about it, and the most rational systems may be used as devices to distract from the reality of what is actually happening.

Other people's experiences are more useful than their solutions

This is about the generalization of findings and their transfer from one situation to another, and whether this is appropriate action.

If we are dealing with a current problem, we might want to see what is available in the literature or in other people's work that might give us a guide to what to do. This aphorism's perspective makes it clear that what is useful is not primarily the grand conclusions that people have come to, but practical details about what they ran up against and how they handled the problems on the way. There is a certain kind of generalization here, but it is something like 'learning from other people's experience'.

In some respects, the worst generalizations are those solutions that have been produced and are then offered for sale. Many people sell training packages and many organizations try to buy in solutions in the way of packages or procedures—for example, the organizational development package, T-group training and grid leadership. Again, as noted under the last aphorism, they are rational systems used as devices for distraction. In this case, they enable people to avoid tackling the real problems.

In trying to get to grips with what the real problems are, we have to cut swathes through thick undergrowth and overgrowth of failures, to look at experience and at attempts to buy in and add on techniques and procedures. Only by such thorough analysis of a situation can the real problems be identified. Only when the real problem is known can appropriate solutions be applied. It is not learning from other people to copy their techniques.

To introduce solutions from somewhere else is to ignore two things:

- the matrix of unique history, experience and expectation into which the solution is implanted;
- the surrounding conditions of both the original and the current situation.

Applying such solutions is closed-system thinking.

Action begins where analysis begins

If a diagnostic analysis begins on the basis of the previous aphorisms—that is to say, working where the problem is, within the discretion to act, clarifying assumptions about expectation and taking feelings and responsibilities into account—then there is a chance of the analysis being itself the beginning of the change process.

This clashes with the traditional idea of analysis leading to recommendation leading to decision-making leading to implementation, especially if it is taken as a linear sequence of discrete steps (a point made a number of times in chapter 6, when discussing the consulting cycle). If analysis is approached with the idea that implementation is three steps away, then it is hardly surprising that implementation appears to be such a difficulty.

It is not only possible but necessary to delete the step of recommendation. Consultant recommendations made without client collaboration are the ones that tend to 'explode' upon implementation: having 'lit the fuse' with recommendations, the consultant would do well to retire immediately! If the client and the consultant are making collaborative analyses of action possibilities, then how can the consultant recommend anything without taking away the client's responsibility? The essence of consulting is working jointly with the client.

Insight is not enough

The political nature of change processes is such that it is possible to understand very well and yet be in the wrong place, to lack the discretion for action, to lack the power to do what you would like about it, or to find that what is being suggested is strongly resisted. A client's insight might not be enough to enable action to occur, because he or she doesn't want it to—maybe because of cost, risk, skill or associated factors.

A consultant is well placed to help a client gain insight, including insight into the political nature of the problem and possible action, but a consultant is not in a position to give power to someone who does not have it. Nor should a consultant attempt to fix a power system in the interest of a client—what happens when the consultant goes?

What can a consultant do to help people to get moving? There is no simple answer, even though there are alternative theoretical models available. It has a lot to do with discovering with the client what the barriers are and what strength of push to action there is, and then working from there.

In this regard, do not pull your punches. This does not mean you should be brash and uncensored, but if you spot a hidden, undeclared or denied aim, an unnoticed effect, an unregarded implication, a fantasy, and if you see it as a barrier to understanding and action, then do not hint at it—name the devil squarely. People usually know anyway, and so articulation of the problem might break the pretence, the collusion, the denial of what is there—the Emperor's new clothes again.

If you can see the key anxiety, act. So often a confused mess of doubts, arguments, figures, forecasts or scenarios may be supported in its confusion by a quite specific fear. Working with a client to find this key fear or anxiety does help in resolving many issues.

Protect the boundary

An awareness of the openness of systems means an awareness of the way in which surrounding circumstances affect the appropriateness of internal arrangements, procedures or states. Putting your head down and carrying on as though the outside world (that beyond the boundary of the section, department or organization) is not changing is to run the risk that the outside world will react in a most unwelcome way—especially if you are not looking behind you at the time.

The pressure to isolate, devitalize or annihilate a consultancy may come as much from envy at its prospective success as from anxiety about its perceived threat to other people's existence and valued ways of working.

The environment contains actors who not only relate to the innovating consultants and clients, but also to each other. In such a richly joined environment, the attack might come from an unexpected and unpredictable direction.

Don't expect the credit

You won't get it!

It may seem that there are so many things that can go wrong, it's a wonder if something goes well. Yet sometimes they do—well enough, anyway—just as some patients get better. However, most consultants of experience know well that credit is very rare indeed.

SMITH'S MANAGEMENT CONSULTING INSIGHTS

The power balance

Because you have no authority in the relationship with clients, you can only influence clients by demonstrating your expertise, developing a common vision, using anticipation and trust, and working on reducing tensions and anxieties. The client–consultant contract is a mutual one and sets out the obligations and responsibilities of both parties. Thus 'who pays the piper calls the tune'—but not if the piper has to compromise on ethics or standards.

Being a consultant is not easy and can, in fact, be frustrating. But it can also be fun and enjoyable simply because it is not logical and predictable. You manage lateral relationships with no authority and with no leverage except your skill, personality and influential ability. The power balance between you and your client is always open to ambiguity and negotiation.

Interest in people

As a consultant, you must be sufficiently interested in people (clients) to get involved in their affairs and sufficiently interested in the problem itself to intervene. A lack of interest in either clients or their problems can lead to cynical and self-serving consultancy.

Diagnosis is the key

You must never take the problem away from the people who own it. It must be left to them to solve, with your consulting help if you are in a position to help. The key to success in this process is diagnosis of the problem (see Table 4, p. 63).

Diagnosis requires a comprehensive examination of the client system in order to establish a working hypothesis about what is being dealt with. In my view, no intervention, whether it be generalist, specialist or a package, will succeed without some degree of diagnosis. As implied in one of Hutton's aphorisms, it is not learning to copy someone else's techniques and just apply them as 'the solution' without diagnosing the situation.

A two-way affair

As noted in chapter 2, giving advice is not consulting. Consulting should be seen as interactive, with knowledge and advice transfer very much a two-way affair.

Practising consultant Richard Farson (1996) elucidates this concept when he states that his advice to consultants is not to take his advice—even though he has a lot of advice to give about the philosophy and methodology of consulting and plenty of solutions to particular problems he has encountered. He explains this paradox in terms of dealing with clients by suggesting that clients should not do as he says. Rather, he gives the following steps for a collaborative effort between consultant and client:

> let us figure out together what to do, then let us do together whatever we concur are the right things to do, given whatever we agree are the potential risks and rewards of the kinds of changes we are considering, in the situation for which we have determined we have the responsibility, the ability, and the resources to do what both of us believe can and should be done.

It is not always easy to follow this consulting approach: there is a strong tendency on the part of the consultant to want to sell his or her own solution because the client is so 'stupid' as not to have seen the right answer yet!

While technique is important, it is even more important to be sensitive to, and in empathy with, the relationship between you and your client. As I have said so often, the problem presented is not usually the causal problem, and helping the client to become aware of this without upsetting the relationship can be a real test of consulting skill.

A flexible approach

It is a mistake to be rigid and inflexible and to approach every organization and every problem in the same way.

The successful approach and solution of the past can be the failure of the present if applied in different circumstances — as stated in the aphorism 'Other people's experiences are more useful than their solutions'. We need to be open, curious and creative and not enamoured of our favourite method or solution.

The more you learn about the operation of organizations and their management and the behaviour of individuals and groups in organizations, the better consultant you will be. Contributing disciplines to the field are sociology, psychology, anthropology, history, politics and philosophy, as well as management and organization theory itself. This knowledge base enables you to operate successfully in whatever functional area the problems exist.

Many people have been involved in treating organizational pain on the basis of interventions that do not adequately take into account the psychology of the individuals involved or a comprehensive conception of what the organization is all about, or do not have the flexibility to adjust to changing situations.

The importance of goodwill

It is often the case that there is not much wrong with the treatment but its application is misunderstood or misapplied. In other words, you have to know what you are doing, and implementation depends almost entirely on the acceptance and goodwill of the people who are involved as either givers or receivers of the treatment.

I often think that good alternative names for a consultant are 'illuminator' and 'reflector'. A good consultant sees his or her role as shedding light on a particular people situation that is experiencing difficulties, or reflecting back to the people in the situation a view of themselves and the situation that they can recognize as representing the general reality of that situation.

As a consultant, you will be evaluated and judged on what you do, how you do it and the results you achieve, rather than on what you say you will do and achieve. However, as one of Hutton's aphorisms claims, don't expect the credit if you succeed.

It is in the nature of people to 'shoot the messenger' who brings bad news, even if it is true (and it's almost a given that consultants will deliver some bad news to some people). However, if the consultant has generated sufficient goodwill during the project, then his or her bad news is likely to be better received. It is also useful to deliver, along with the bad news, some comment on the positive aspects of the project and the benefits that will accrue from fixing the problems.

Your actions as a consultant will provide evidence to clients about your assumptions, beliefs and standards. In this regard you have to ensure that you measure up to the standards you claim, or that are expected of a consultant, and the beliefs and values you espouse.

Change and resistance

Causing change is the essence of consulting. Without the accomplishment of change, it can be a parasitic profession. Edgar Schein (1969), the 'creator' of process consulting, says that if you really want to understand something, try to change it.

Along with this assertion, it should be acknowledged that organizations and people must be ready to change or prepared to change—in other words, the present pain must be such that change becomes a necessity rather than an option. In many circumstances, the conditional pressure for change occurs only when there is a nexus of three forces: pressure from the top, pressure from inside and pressure from outside.

Machiavelli (1950) expresses the basis for resistance to change very well. He notes that nothing is more difficult to carry out, nor more doubtful of success, nor more difficult to manage than to initiate a new order of things. This is because the initiator has the enmity of all who profit by preservation of the old system, and merely lukewarm defenders in those who would gain by the new one.

Future change

The future will not be a continuation of the past. It will be a series of discontinuities, and linear thinking in such a non-linear world will be useless. For challenging and stimulating views on the nature of that future, a read of *Rethinking the Future* (Gibson 1997) is recommended. This text contains articles by luminaries who are recognized as leading business thinkers—including Charles Handy, Stephen Covey, Gary Hamel, Warren Bennis, Peter Senge, Michael Porter and Philip Kotler.

Their contributions aim at defining the new paradigm that will revolutionize business and society in the twenty-first century. Consultants would do well to be thinking about how that new paradigm will affect how they do their job and help organizations in coming years.

The next chapter presents some challenging views that confront past principles and practices, and provide some pointers to the future.

11 Contrary views and final thoughts on consulting

This chapter discusses some controversial ideas and views that challenge the approach to management consulting generally advocated in this book, and includes some final thoughts on the consulting process.

CONTRARY VIEWS

Quantification as camouflage

Despite my insistence that the process of consulting is not certain, linear, analytical or quantitative, it is difficult for people to accept this fact when our main approach to education concentrates on these factors and preconditions us to operate in this way. Kevin Kelly (in Gibson 1997) suggests that the increasing complexity of organizations and the big improvements in communication technology will result in networking becoming the dominating organizational mode of operation. Essentially, a network is a decentralized organism that has no hard boundaries, no centre and no head. The causes of events within its sphere are not linear. A causes B causes C causes D, but then D causes A—that is, there is a field of causes rather than a series of linear causes.

This idea should perhaps be kept in mind when applying the traditional approach set out in chapter 6 in the section on problem analysis and synthesis.

Consulting is, in reality, a much more uncertain, qualitative, creative and intuitive process than it may appear. As Albert Einstein is said to have noted: 'I never came upon any of my discoveries through the process of rational thinking'.

Alistair Mant (1997) notes that the mantra of the quantitative people is 'If you can't measure it, you can't manage it'. He then questions the wisdom of this mantra by saying that even the guru of statistical process control, W. Edwards Deming, understood that the things that really matter like love, generosity, trust, courage, integrity and happiness resist calibration.

In other forums, I have heard this mantra criticized as 'quantification as camouflage'. Two books worth reading as antitheses to the current 'technophilia' are those by Clifford Stoll (1995) and Theodore Roszak (1994). Both authors suggest that technology has generated plenty of human contact but not much humanity; that the computer is a metaphor, not a living experience.

Neither man is a Luddite, but, as both suggest, real life and authentic experience mean much more than anything a modem can deliver. Computers and associated quantitative techniques have added great value to our lives but only through adding another dimension to that life, not as a substitute for life's qualitative aspects.

In a similar vein, responses to questions relating to feelings and views can be quantified (usually on some form of Likert scale) and the analysis left to a computer program, which can, of course, give the results an appearance of credibility. However, it is often a case of 'garbage in, gospel out' unless care is taken to verify the findings using other techniques.

As I have found to my cost on a number of occasions when using a survey, turning the respondents' 'felt score' into a quantitative set of measures and subjecting them to all sorts of statistical tests can give the appearance of solidity to pure wind (Winnicott 1974).

Arthur Koestler (1959, p. 534) also criticized this phenomenon when he noted that

> the reduction of quality to quantity (colour, sound radiation etc to vibrational frequencies and human values to raw scores) has meant

that we can measure results but we do not know what is being measured. All we do know in fact is that we read our instruments—the number of clicks on a Geiger counter, the position of a pointer on a dial or the position of a tick on a Likert scale—and interpret the signs according to the rules of the game. The quantities have as much resemblance to qualities as a telephone number has to a subscriber!

The latest 'snake oils'

Two current performance improvement techniques—empowerment and re-engineering—deserve a little adverse publicity, given their wide acceptance, application and claims of success.

Empowerment has had a wide hearing in the management periodicals and textbooks since the early 1990s. The claims associated with empowerment relate to its capacity to maximize the potential of people and organizations and thus to contribute to organizational success. The more fervent of the claims suggest that empowering staff will unleash the synergistic, creative energy of everyone in the organization, and that existing walls and boundaries will fall and fear in the workplace will disappear.

In a recent empirical study, Bill Harley (1998) suggests that empowerment is a myth and that his finding that empowerment has failed to enhance employee autonomy can be attributed to the fact that organizational power resides primarily in the organizational structure. The hierarchy is alive and well, in his view, and remains central to the majority of contemporary organizations, and the impact of other changes to work organization must be understood in this context.

He claims that although many of the empowerment concepts and associated techniques have merit, they do not work when:

- they are used to address the wrong issues;
- they are applied as a global solution to all an organization's problems or improvement efforts;
- they are used without a thorough diagnosis of the particular organization's context and culture;
- they are not given the time and effort required to institutionalize them;

- the outside 'experts' who are called upon to implement them are not prepared to adjust 'the grand plan' to a particular organizational reality.

As Peter Senge (in Gibson 1997) claims, managers hear that they should empower people and so they push decisions out into the organization. However, when things get tough, they pull them right back because they are terrified that pretty soon they might not have any work.

A European study (Coulson-Thomas 1997) into the reasons for the failure of attempts by many big organizations to transform themselves by using various techniques such as restructuring and re-engineering suggests that such failures are due to, among other things:

- a naive faith in a single solution;
- lack of awareness of all options;
- standard methodologies being applied in a different context;
- a focus on 'hard' things and not people;
- a failure to see things through and to see consequences;
- naive faith in the linearity of activity;
- the loss of individual expertise when 'teams' become the norm.

In regard to team building, we should also note the words of John Harvey-Jones (1988, p. 97), an English industrialist:

> teams of superstars, each outstanding in their own area, seldom win because their ability to analyse and criticise is high and their vanity and intelligence frequently make them bad listeners. Each finds it hard to accept any compromise in their own area of knowledge.
>
> Abandoning the purity of a position they know is right is extraordinarily difficult and belief in the importance of the shared aim is not high enough to make the sacrifice worth while.

An article in the *Harvard Business Review* by Jon Katzenbach (1997) says that too often, teamwork becomes a 'feel good' mechanism that can get in the way of anything actually being accomplished.

Other failures—and consultants' contributions to them

Alistair Mant (1997) presents some good reasons for the long-term failure of privatization, delayering and downsizing activities—reasons related to an organization being treated like a mechanical system, a bicycle, rather than a frog, an integrated, living system.

He adds management consultants to his reasons for the failures of such activities. They are, he claims, among the army of 'change agents' (academics included) who in fact feed off instability and change. Their *unconscious* project is to destabilize systems, because stabilization is the source of their power and wealth.

He suggests that these people are persuasive because they are attuned to chaos and deeply believe in the need for incessant change. A change agent, in the sense he uses the term in this context, can be defined as 'an individual with a pathological need to create external chaos commensurate with his or her internal state'.

In other words, he is suggesting that the change industry is sometimes part of the problem rather than part of the solution.

Mant is exaggerating for the sake of emphasis, but perhaps he does have a point.

C. K. Prahalad (in Gibson 1997) says that downsizing can be like corporate anorexia—it can make an organization leaner and thinner but not necessarily healthier. There is a need to build future muscle, not just to cut corporate fat.

Peddling tribal medicine

I attended a conference recently (National Business Education and Research Conference, 14–15 October 1999, Perth, Western Australia, organized by Curtin University of Technology), the theme of which was the management of the interfaces between research, education and business. The keynote speaker was Dr Nan Stone, past editor of the *Harvard Business Review*, who highlighted the difficulties that academic researchers have in communicating with business and vice versa. One questioner encapsulated a view that is probably not uncommon among academics, by asking how Dr Stone felt about the prostitution of academic research at the hands of template consultants. She agreed that it can and does happen, but thought that in most cases, consultants act as an effective bridge between theory and practice.

John Micklethwait and Adrian Woolridge (1996) deliver another broadside at consultants by suggesting that consulting firms, business school professors and management gurus are sales representatives for an industry that exists exclusively to peddle freshly laid management advice to petrified executives. Much modern management theory, they claim, is no more reliable than tribal medicine.

Despite this hatchet job, the authors do spend a lot of time with a scalpel, removing the more outrageous ideas from what is a solid core of useful management theory that can help consultants and managers alike.

I also like to keep in mind a saying I heard many years ago: 'Knowing the answer does not necessarily solve the problem'. The answer has to be put into action and, as I have implied in chapter 6, the process of selling and implementing a solution can be more difficult than coming up with it in the first place.

Humour with a message

The following tongue-in-cheek executive summary of a work study consultant's report (anonymous, of course) on improving the performance of a symphony orchestra has some messages about the tendency of people to try to quantify everything and aim for efficiency and forget effectiveness:

- For considerable periods the four oboe players had nothing to do—the numbers should be reduced and the work spread more evenly over the whole of the concert, thus eliminating peaks of activity.
- All the violins, twelve in number, were playing identical notes—this seems unnecessary duplication. These staff numbers should be cut drastically and if more volume of sound is required it could be obtained by means of electronic amplification.
- Much effort was expended in the playing of demi-semi quavers—this appears to be an unnecessary refinement and it

is recommended that all notes should be rounded up to the nearest semi-quaver. If this were done it would be possible to employ trainees or lower graded employees more extensively.

- There seems to be too much repetition of some musical passages. e.g. no useful purpose is served by repeating on the horns a passage which has already been handled by the strings. It is estimated that if all the redundant passages were eliminated the whole concert time of two hours could be reduced to twenty minutes and there would be no need to waste time on intermission.

- On methods there are several criticisms where engineering principles could be successfully employed. It was noted that the pianist was carrying out his work as a two handed job and was also using both feet for pedal operations, but in spite of this it was noted that some notes called for excessive reaching and it is suggested that the keyboard could be redesigned to bring the notes within the normal working area. In many cases the operators were using only one hand for holding their instruments—a suitable jig could be designed to render the idle hand available for other work. It was also noticed that excessive effort was being used at times by the players of wind instruments, whereas the provision of a small blower fan could provide all the necessary air under more accurately controlled conditions.

- Obsolescence of equipment is another matter of concern as it was noted in the programme that the leading violinist's instrument was already several hundred years old. If normal depreciation had been employed, this instrument could have been written off and more modern equipment purchased.

The foregoing suggestions were discussed with the management in the person of the Conductor but he was of the opinion that the implementation would probably affect the box office. He, of course, has great difficulty defending his position because it involves nothing more than waving a baton at the orchestra members who already have the score in front of them and could perform adequately without his distracting movements.

In the circumstances I have discounted his comments and suggest that, even if the box office is affected, I am sure the great savings arising from putting my recommendations into effect would cancel out any losses caused by lower attendance.

Barry Smith (1996), in an equally facetious set of comments, reflects the plea of a disenchanted manager who is looking for a creative human resource person who can help with his continuous improvement process:

> We have done all the textbook stuff. We've gone back to the knitting, waged marketing warfare and loved our customers to death. We've delayered, devolved, decentralised, outplaced and outsourced.
>
> We are so lean and mean, the skeleton almost jingles as it walks. Quality is an addiction and we are always just in time. Our value chain is gold plated and our processes are so finely re-engineered you could shave with them. We benchmark everything (even the cafe bar) and if it moves we measure it.
>
> So why aren't things working better?

FINAL THOUGHTS

The need for change

In my view, the main task of the consultant is to help clients diagnose the nature of performance problems and their base causes. Knowing where the organization is now is a crucial first step in tackling the issues associated with deciding where the client wants it to be and how it is going to get there.

If consultants who purport to help organizations improve performance were aware of the traps specified and implied by the iconoclasts noted earlier in this chapter, then the profession would be less liable to criticism and the successes would receive more publicity than they seem to now.

In a recent newspaper article, Gary Younge (1999) suggests that the consultants of the 1970s to the 1980s were an army of overpaid 'suits', equipped with flip charts, laptops and baffling jargon and with a mission to downsize, right size and re-engineer firms into peak profitability. In their wake, he says, they have left a trail of redundancies and managers afraid to manage. He mentions one of the gurus of the management consulting world, Tom Peters, co-author of *In Search of Excellence*, and notes that two-thirds of the companies Peters cited as examples of excellence have run into trouble. He claims that when his theory seemed to have been disproved by reality, Peters remarked, 'My principles have survived intact—it's just that the companies haven't'.

However, the times and consultants are 'a-changing'. Younge notes that the thrust in consulting now is away from concentrating simply on profit, cost and revenue to focusing on ideas and creativity and growth. To get an edge on competitors in the current (and future) business climate, companies are turning to innovative ideas and intellectual capital, and so consultants with a lively imagination are more valuable than those who have a well-educated brain and a safe pair of hands.

There is no doubt that management consulting is a controversial profession (or job) and that there are many differing views as to its application and to its successes and failures.

However, as I said at the beginning of this book, and will conclude in my final chapter, it generates very big money and is growing rapidly as an industry. Younge quotes figures claiming that there are now a quarter of a million management consultants worldwide, that the profession is growing by 16 per cent per year and that 90 per cent of Britain's top 300 companies employed outside consultants in 1998.

Traps for players

The following list of traps for players in the organization development field, and for change agents, may be useful, even though it adds to, or reinterprets, the already formidable list of 'don'ts' and 'traps' presented previously in one form or another in this book. The list is attributed to Australian behavioural scientist Dexter Dunphy:

- *Assuming a change is needed:* 'I'm giving you artificial resuscitation—don't keep getting up'.
- *Inappropriate use of behavioural versus structural interventions:* Is a 'personality clash' a function of poor human skills or poor role clarity?
- *Attempting bottom-up change:* Remember the military dictum—the penalty for mutiny is death!

- *Creating change overload:* We want to change your attitude, your work methods, and your leadership style—by next month.
- *Raising expectations beyond what is possible:* From the start, think and talk in terms of three to four years.
- *Inappropriate attachment:* 'Do you want me to be servant, master, captive behavioural scientist, visiting professor, tame seal or resident magician?'
- *Becoming trapped in one part/changing only a subsystem:* This can occur with subsystems aligned horizontally or vertically.
- *Losing professional detachment:* Liking the client, wanting the client to like you, wanting the intervention to be a great success, attempting to impress the client, getting joy from praise—watch out!
- *Using the package plan, whatever the problem—identified properly or not:* 'I don't know for sure what your problem is but management by objectives will cure it!'
- *The myth of complete objectivity:* Don't fool yourself into thinking you are completely objective—it is impossible to be.

I hope all this does not put you off consulting forever! Providing you are aware of the traps and how to avoid them, and follow sound consulting practice with regard to the cycle and project management, your chances of success are high.

An ending

12

Having reached the conclusion of my current thoughts about consulting, I will end on a positive note in regard to the career of consultancy.

I obtain great satisfaction from being a management consultant but I recognize that it is not everyone's 'cup of tea'. The highs achieved by delivering the 'goods' to a client have to be balanced with the lows that can come from the uncertainty of work, the lack of security, the unreliability of client assistance, the lack of executive power to influence situations, and the 'crushed' feeling you get when your work is rejected.

The challenge for those wishing to pursue a consulting career is to correctly identify personal skills, to investigate the market for those skills, to determine the demand for them and to stimulate the market to want to use you as the supplier.

Consultants already in business find that they need to be doing this on a continuing basis, as the business world is never static. Keeping in touch with the market and what clients want is the only way to keep up. The price of complacency—offering the same old solutions and failing to change methods and style—can be high.

Consulting has become an expanding function in the business world, because of the following factors:

- The rapid development of technology and the increasing complexity of business and society in general. Managers in organizations are finding it more and more difficult to be able to master all the variables that impact on their performance and so are turning to consultants for assistance more than in the past.

- People problems seem to be creating organizational crises that are more evident than in the past and which cannot be treated by remedies that worked in a more authoritarian era. These problems relate to such things as underutilization of staff, misuse of people's talents, lack of confidence in management and uncertainties in regard to job security. This is fertile ground for management consultants in the human resources management area.

- Organizational changes that are implemented as solutions, such as downsizing, privatization, decentralization and mergers, have created problems that have not existed before, and the outside consultant, who often plays a role in these changes, can find further work in helping managers to tackle these unforeseen consequences.

- Many opportunities are now arising in sectors of society that have not been traditional users of consultancy services—for example, non-profit, religious, recreational and sporting associations and organizations.

The IMC benchmark study conducted in Western Australia makes the following final comments, which are interesting in the context of my 'ending':

> The current moves to privatise sectors of government operations in Western Australia and demand for leaner government will result in a freeing up of activities and services from the public to private sector and conversely a greater demand will arise for services that only governments are best placed to provide.
>
> Hence while the public sector has already become a major user of management consulting services, it is not unrealistic to predict that it will remain a growth market for consultants in years to come. The quality of work, reliability, level of service to the client and good relationships with the client will be particularly important for both client and consultant. Clients will seek out consultants whose profiles match special process and/or sector criteria and who exhibit a 'track record'.

The increasing complexity of consulting assignments in terms of problem solving, client/consultant relationships, competitive cost-value estimations, longer term consulting, business vision and growth/viability, will probably require a variety of different management approaches, to meet the clients' perceived and actual needs. One such approach that has been gaining recognition amongst professionals and management researchers, eager to develop more coherent theory and practice systems for solving all manner of problems, is systemic or systems thinking. This approach is particularly relevant in circumstances where consultants at present are not able to convincingly demonstrate the value adding contribution (not just the cost recovery) they have made to the organisation contracting them.

The trend towards the formation of strategic alliances in today's globally competitive business environment will also be an increasingly visible feature of the way business is done and the consulting industry will not be immune to this practice eg. formation of project specific consortiums (which then disband at the end of the project).

As previously noted, anecdotal and some research evidence suggests that clients are not always happy with consultant services. Given this sometimes poor record of results in the client–consultant relationship, there is a need for those involved, from both sides, to learn more about the nature of the process and how it can be applied in an efficient and effective manner.

Most failures, I suspect, come about because of misunderstanding about the nature of the consulting cycle and the roles of consultant and client, and because of the differing expectations of the contract activities and results.

There are no simple procedural answers towards solving organizational dilemmas or moving them from an 'is' to an 'ought' state—hence the need for clarifying the expectations of both sides in a consulting contract, the development of trust between both sides and the working through of the contract in a collaborative manner.

When these needs are met, then there is a high probability that the consultant and the client will produce a result that could well exceed their expectations because of the synergy generated by the sound matching of outside expertise and inside skill and knowledge.

Much of what I have said in this book is not new, but I have presented it in a new way. The words have been said before; you can find plenty of them by looking at the material listed in appendix B, for example. The main difference is whether or not my way of presentation enables you to understand them, relate to them and act on them. In this regard, I hope that I have reached you, whether you are a potential consultant, a consultant, a client or an employee in an organization that is the subject of a consulting intervention.

APPENDIX A   Case study exercises

CLIENT–CONSULTANT SITUATIONS

The following situations give you a chance to discuss issues, assumptions, beliefs and values, and procedures in regard to the client–consultant relationship and consulting as a process.

For each you are asked to:

- decide what the issues for the consultant are;
- decide what the issues for the client are;
- consider the implications of the situation for the project and what should be done now.

Fairness and equity in a method study contract

A consultant puts in a proposal to undertake a two-month fixed-term consultancy to investigate the efficiency and effectiveness of the purchasing department in a large organization. The CEO of the organization rings the consultant to say that she can have the job if the proposed fee is reduced by $5,000 to $27,000.

Conflicting results from information generation methods in a human resources management contract

In the process of generating information from employees about morale in an organization, a consultant uses two methods: personal interviews and a survey of the same respondents. The results, to the consultant's dismay, are almost the opposite of each other—the interviews indicate low morale and the survey indicates satisfactory morale.

Political influence on a human resource development consulting report

A consultant puts in a preliminary final report to a government department after an evaluation assignment that looked at the costs and benefits of a new program to train skilled workers in the hospitality industry. The department's assignment manager rings the consultant to say that the negative tone of the report must be watered down considerably before it can be presented to the minister concerned.

The manager sends a long list of changes to the consultant, along with an amended executive summary that paints a rosier view of the new program than does the consultant's.

A management consulting situation where the problem is the client

It is near the middle of an assignment in which the consultant has been called in to do an organizational analysis to ascertain why, as the client CEO claims, there are so many problems with middle management decision-making—the managers are just not making decisions without checking everything out with him. After examining the situation, the consultant becomes convinced that the main problems in this area of management emanate from the CEO himself. The CEO is her client and she has to decide what to do next.

Ethics in contracting/subcontracting on an information technology consultancy

An organization asks a consultant to put in a proposal for a job to install a computer-based accounting package named by the organization's accountant. The consultant is familiar with the package and suspects that it is not the most suitable for the organization concerned. At the time, the consultant is inundated with work but does have a network of consultant contacts, some of whom are available to help. He decides to put in a proposal for the work and name one of his contacts as his associate in the project.

Fairness in awarding a contract

A government department is asking for quotations for a consultancy to examine how the concept of intellectual capital (IC) measurement and management can be introduced to the department. It has a consultant (James Morley, from a small local consulting firm) already working for it on a project that involves determining the key performance indicators that can be used to measure overall output effectiveness. This project is nearly complete and they have been impressed with James's work.

Management would like to award the IC contract to James but has to follow procedure and call for quotations from other consultants.

Three other consulting firms put in quotations. One of those firms, ENTECH Ltd, has a track record in IC work and considers that it has a good chance to win the contract. The contract is awarded to James Morley. ENTECH director Fred Harvey hears from a contact in the department that the awarding of the contract to Morley was a foregone conclusion. Fred complains to the department head, who tells him that the correct procedures have been followed and the contract has been awarded to the best quotation.

Identifying the problem

A company CEO calls in a consultant and tells him that over the past year sales have been falling and internal information sharing between production and sales, as well as customer relations problems, seems to be at the core of the poor results. He asks the consultant to design and run a training program on communication for his sales and production staff, aimed at giving them a better understanding of the process and its most effective application. The consultant queries whether in fact the answer is training and raises the point that other factors could well be causing the difficulties described by the CEO. He asks whether he could be contracted to spend a week in the company, looking at its operation, and talking to key people inside and outside the organization in order to identify clearly the core problem. The response from the

CEO is: 'Look, I know what the problem is, it's poor communication, and I have asked you here to give me a quote on the design and running of a course on communication, not to pay for you to wander around talking to people about their jobs and problems'.

Secret surveys

A consultant decides to use an attitude survey to gather information in relation to a project he has undertaken to determine the level of morale in an organization. When the consultant has used the survey previously, he has been careful to ensure that no respondent can be identified and thus there is more chance of obtaining true opinions and feelings. The client agrees to his request to include this means of information gathering in the project. However, he asks the consultant to use a secret identifying code on each survey so that he not only will get truer results but will also be able to identify who the 'problem' staff are.

A billing issue

In the course of a consulting visit to another city, in which a consultant has two clients, he is involved in providing services to both. His expenses include travel, accommodation and out-of-pocket payments. In deciding how to bill the clients for expenses, he considers that trying to pro rata these for each client could cause questions from their accountants, as each client is unaware that he consults to the other. To make it easier on himself and them, he bills both for the entire expense amount.

A client's hidden agenda

As part of a project brief to investigate the strategy, structure and performance of a company, a consultant is required to interview all the second- and middle-level managers. With the results of the interviews and other information, the consultant writes a report presenting a synthesis of the information and a set of recommendations for future joint action. The company CEO reads the report and then asks the consultant for a brief written report on his view of each of the managers interviewed, as he wants to get a better idea of their strengths and weaknesses in order to help them improve their performance. The consultant complies with the request. A few weeks after he has completed the project and left the company, he hears that three of the managers have been fired on the basis of his interview reports.

A CASE STUDY SCENARIO

Although this case is based on a company operating in the 1980s, the issues have not become outdated by the passage of time. Many small, family-owned enterprises operating today could be used to illustrate similar issues of concern.

Company profile

Westside Products was originally founded in Western Australia in the late 1940s and continues to operate through a holding company whose shares are still family owned, mainly by two brothers. Other family members hold the remaining shares. There is a board consisting of shareholders, but it is not active in directing the company.

The company business is shopfitting, window manufacturing and glass merchandising, and generally profits have been made over the years, even in difficult times.

It is well known locally as an old, established firm with a reputation for high-quality work at reasonable prices.

The company still relies on the same products as it did twenty years ago, and the employer–employee relationship is very much one of master–servant.

The solid base for the company is its core of long-serving, loyal employees, but this base is being eroded by retirements.

In recent months, there has been increased union activity in the factory, and higher wage costs and a more competitive environment are putting pressure on the company's profitability.

The company has been a glass merchant since the 1960s and this has been a very profitable area, although the boom years resulting from high-rise development in the 1970s and early 1980s have gone, and the market is now relatively stable.

The largest output areas of the factory, and the oldest, are the cabinets and metalwork sections, where all types of carpentry work and metal fitting are carried out. The profit margin on much of this work is low, as it is subject to the tendering system.

However, because of Westside's good name, some work is received automatically, and on this type of job, a reasonable margin can be obtained.

Early in 1987, the manager of the company completed a deal with an Eastern States firm to buy aluminium window sections from that firm and assemble and sell them in Western Australia. The use of Westside's glass in the windows would help boost glass sales. After the deal was done, a preliminary survey of the window market was not encouraging, as it showed that it was well served by existing products.

By March 1987, a salesman had been hired and raw materials purchased.

Westside has always been owned by the one family, and the present general manager, John Homes, is a particularly forceful person, being a dominating force both in the company and in the family. He spends only three to six months of the year in Western Australia and in the remainder of the time he resides in the United Kingdom.

The company founder (John's grandfather) had a 'shirtsleeves' approach to his business, and he brought together a group of quality tradesmen, many of whom are still with the company, although a good number are now reaching retirement age.

John is a well-qualified engineer and has a knack of annoying people because he makes it obvious that he considers himself superior and the 'master' of the company.

The actual manager on a daily basis is Bob Fields, who has resigned himself to having to manage within quite serious constraints in regard to the more important policy decisions.

Bob, however, is himself an autocratic manager and makes quick decisions with little or no staff input. What he wants done gets done, even though he operates a lot on 'gut feeling', which makes him unpredictable.

Jim Casey, the glass factory manager, believes that his department is the only part of the company of value and hence does not cooperate with other managers and frequently clashes with them over operational and financial matters.

Bob has nine people reporting to him but communicates often with staff below that level. (See Figure A.1 for the company organization and p. 159 for thumbnail sketches of the main personalities.)

Both the glass and the general factory managers have direct control over their employees. In the general factory, there is no formal hierarchy, but an informal system exists in which the older men take responsibility — though leadership changes from job to job.

The tendency in the office is also to run to an informal system. While this works well for the long-term employees, new employees have problems in finding out what should be done and difficulty in establishing work schedules and priorities. The estimating function is particularly uncoordinated and is considered to be somewhat of a 'black art' able to be carried out only by the old hands.

The financial figures (see Table A.1) indicate that for the 1986–87 year, the company made a nominal profit of $232,710 on sales of $2,626,140. However, as can also be seen, when work in progress is taken into account, the real return for the year's work is only $27,417. Most of the work-in-progress figure adjustment applies to the carpentry and metalwork area, so the $167,640 profit shown for that area is not a true reflection of its performance.

The windows section has only been operating since February 1987 and a number of technical difficulties have had to be overcome in the initial stages of assembly. The salesman has been finding it hard to break into the market and at this time (August 1987) only two builders are consistent buyers. The initial loss was anticipated, but the three-year forecast is also pessimistic. This forecast is the first done by the company for any of its products, because sales prediction has in the past been considered too hard an exercise by the sales staff. The windows section forecast is also based on a 1987–88 overall budget, the first produced by the company, at the instigation of the new accountant. Accounting was previously done by an external firm and dealt with historical figures only.

The stock of window raw materials is high, at $120,000. This has occurred because of the need to stock both metric and imperial lengths of aluminium and because of high expectations of market penetration. The lead time for ordering this material is two to three weeks.

Stocks of glass are valued at $119,802. At the current rate of consumption, there is a year and a half's supply of glass. There is also an unvalued $30,000 (not shown in the financial figures) worth of useable cut glass sheets. The difficulty of ordering glass is that it has to be ordered in minimum container quantities and the lead time on orders can be one to four months.

The carpentry/metalwork stores stock of $142,620 is mainly made up of aluminium, stainless steel and timber of various sorts. The value appears high, given that most of the items are over-the-counter purchasable items. Bulk purchasing obviously keeps the unit cost down but at the expense of keeping a high value of stock.

The difficulty of evaluating the cost of excessive stock is that continual price rises can reward the overstocker more than if the stocks were kept low and the saved money invested.

Figures show varied results from each section. There is a particular concern in the carpentry and metalwork section, as jobs recently completed there, originally estimated by recent appointee Joe Fenton, have been showing extremely low contributions. These problem jobs were won by successful tender. Investigation has shown that labour estimates have not been met in the factory. The factory manager feels that the times allowed were ridiculous.

The present situation seems to be of a company trading on its good name, which has been won by a loyal group of employees, but morale is not high because of poor results, impending retirements, and union questions and involvement in matters such as wages and conditions.

The present factory is being fully utilized and it is impossible to develop the site any further. It is likely that within the next few years, the property will be subject to a government compulsory purchase order.

The personalities

General manager, John Homes: John is 54 years old and his home is now in the United Kingdom, where he went after recruiting Bob Fields to take his place as manager. He is a quick thinker and very able in the engineering field. He can be extremely rude and is generally disliked, perhaps even feared, by the staff of the operating company. His visits usually create disruption and disharmony among staff, but they are obliged to follow his general policy line.

Manager, Bob Fields: Bob is 54 years old and has been with the company for three years. He is a heavy smoker and a more than occasional drinker. He can be unpredictable—for example, sometimes he is approachable and open to discussion, but on other occasions he is impetuous and becomes angry over trivial issues. He tends to be autocratic and hasty in his decision-making. Before coming to Westside, he had a responsible job as production manager in a rival firm, where his performance record was very good.

Sales manager, Michael Wilkinson: Mike is 49 years old and has been with the company for thirty years. His client contacts are invaluable and he starts work late and is relatively heavy on his expense account. He has an overbearing attitude and a superior manner. Mike's work is highly effective but he makes no attempt to manage his sales team, the four estimators.

Estimator 1, Matthew Hobbs: He is due to retire this coming Christmas, having started with the company as a young man. The work he obtains is profitable and he works long hours and is one of the mainstays of the firm. He has an easygoing and pleasant personality and is liked and respected by all staff.

Estimator 2, Tony Lehman: Tony is 55 years old and has been with the company for twenty years. He recently underwent a serious operation, from which he has recovered. His attitude over recent months has been slack, and he tends to spend more time away from the office, with fewer results.

Estimator 3, Joe Fenton: Joe is 40 and has been with the company for seven months. He is something of a playboy and is not settling in well, and pays little attention to the manager's instructions. A number of contracts for which he has successfully tendered have been losses when manufactured. He considers that it is the antiquated methods and poor and congested work conditions that contribute to the losses, and not his estimating.

Window estimator and salesman, Carl Pizzalli: Carl is 35 and a real salesperson who has been with the company for seven months and is confident and brash. His private life is a mess, with debts and separation from his wife and children. This has at times affected his work and he is having a hard time getting into the window market. He is away from the office for days on end and there have been questions as to whether he is working or not.

Draftsman, Peter Homes: Peter, 21 years old, is a member of the family who owns the company, and son of the general factory manager. He is a good worker in many ways but has a knack of making mistakes that can cost money. He has little concentration and is generally used as a driver and a measurer of jobs. At the end of November 1987, he is leaving on a six-month holiday to the United Kingdom.

Accountant, Patrick Scott: Patrick is 30 and has been with the company for seven months. He has expressed concerns about the state of the company. He dislikes the manager and feels over-qualified for the job he is doing because it is clerical, with little responsibility. Getting the company to establish a budget was a major achievement, but he is not sure it will be used. A computer operator reports to him and, although very efficient, she says that she intends leaving for personal reasons early in the new year. The telephonist appears to report to him but this is not clear, as everyone is in contact with her. She is 30 and gives every indication of never budging from the job. Patrick was taken aback when he started and saw the old-style factory layout and the equipment and materials jumbled together. He could not see how such an apparently chaotic and unsystematic factory operation could produce the quality products it does.

Factory manager — general, Ernie Homes: Ernie is 50 years old and John's younger brother. He has been in the company factory all his working life, rising up from a trades position. He appears to be an effective manager. The jobs go out on time, to a good quality standard, and the employees are kept working in a fairly happy environment. Many of his workers have been with him for years.

Factory manager—glass, Jim Casey: Jim is 54 and has been with the company for thirty years. He is called the 'mother', as he rarely lets any of his workers do anything on their own.

Company organization charts

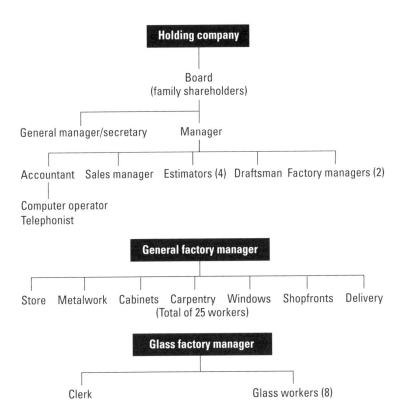

Figure A.1   Westside Products—company organization

Financial figures

Table A.1   Westside Products—financial figures 1986–87

	Total	Carpentry/metalwork	Glass	Windows
Sales	2,626,140	2,079,819	495,000	51,321
COS (materials)	749,235	629,343	89,100	30,792
COS (labour)	621,552	543,060	74,250	4,242
Contribution	1,255,353	907,416	331,650	16,287
Factory costs	452,484	304,617	134,367	13,500
Admin. costs	570,159	435,159	117,000	18,000
Profit (before tax)	232,710	167,640	80,283	(15,213)
Raw material stock				
30/6/87	382,422	142,620	119,802	120,000
30/6/86	170,247	77,970	92,277	–

Profit figure adjusted for work in progress (WIP)

	Year end	Less WIP	Plus WIP	Adjusted figures
	30/6/87	30/6/86	30/6/87	30/6/87
Sales	2,626,140	−729,234	+288,300	2,185,206
COS	1,370,787	−437,541	+201,900	1,135,146
Contrib.	1,255,353	−291,693	+86,400	1,050,060
Factory exp.	452,484			452,484
Admin. exp.	570,159			570,159
Profit	232,710			27,417

APPENDIX B   Further reading

ADDITIONAL BOOKS/ARTICLES OF POSSIBLE INTEREST

Akerlof, G. A. (1970), 'The market for "lemons": Qualitative uncertainty and the market mechanism', *Quarterly Journal of Economics*, 84, 488–500.

Ashford, M. (1998), *Con Tricks: The Shadowy World of Management Consultancy and How to Make it Work for You*, Simon & Schuster, London.

Bain, J. S. (1968), *Industrial Organization*, 2nd edn, John Wiley, New York.

Batstone, S. J. (1991), 'New business service firms: An exploratory study', in L. G. Davies & A. A. Gibb (eds), *Recent Research in Entrepreneurship*, Avebury, Aldershot.

Beer, M., Eisenstat, R. & Spector, B. (1988), *The Critical Path to Change: Developing the Competitive Organization*, Harvard Business School Press, Boston.

Bennett, R. (1990), *Choosing and Using Management Consultants*, Kogan Page, New York.

Biswas, Sugata & Twitchell, Daryl (1999), *Management Consulting: A Complete Guide to the Industry*, John Wiley, New York.

Blake, R. R. & Mouton, J. S. (1983), *Consultation: A Handbook for Individual and Organizational Development*, Addison-Wesley, Reading.

Bloomfield, B. P. & Best, A. (1992), 'Management consultants: Systems development, power and the translation of problems', *Sociological Review*, 40, 533–60.

Bloomfield, B. P. & Danieli, A. (1995), 'The role of management consultants in the development of information technology: The indissoluble nature of socio-political and technical skills', *Journal of Management Studies*, 32, 23–46.

Bryson, J., Keeble, D. & Wood, P. (1993), 'The creation, location and growth of small business service firms in the United Kingdom', *Service Industries Journal*, 13, 118–31.

Buchanan, D. & Boddy, D. (1992), *The Expertise of the Change Agent: Public Performance and Backstage Activity*, Prentice Hall, London.

Clark, I. & Clark, T. (1990), 'Personal management and the use of executive recruitment consultancies', *Human Resource Management Journal*, 1, 46–62.

Clark, T. (1993), 'The market provision of management services, information asymmetries and service quality: Some market solutions: An empirical example', *British Journal of Management*, 4, 235–51.

—— (1993), *Headhunters of Enterprise: Executive Search and Selection Consultancies*, Small Business Research Trust Business Services Research monograph no. 1, School of Management, The Open University, Milton Keynes.

Clark, T. & Mabey, C. (1994), 'The changing use of executive recruitment consultancies by client companies, 1989–1993', *Journal of General Management*, 20, 42–54.

Clark, T. & Salaman, G. (1995), 'Understanding consultancy as performance: The dramaturgical metaphor', in I. Glover & M. Hughes (eds), *Professions at Bay*, Gower, Aldershot.

Coleman, J. S. (1988), 'Social capital in the creation of human capital', *American Journal of Sociology*, 94 (supplement), S95–S120.

Czarniawska-Joerges, B. (1990), 'Merchants of meaning: Managing consulting in the Swedish public sector', in B. Turner (ed.), *Organizational Symbolism*, De Gruyter, New York, 139–50.

Dawes, P. C., Dowling, G. R. & Patterson, P. G. (1992), 'Criteria used to select management consultants', *Industrial Marketing Management*, 21, 187–93.

Drucker, P. (1988), 'The coming of the new organization', *Harvard Business Review*, January–February, 45–53.

Dwyer, R. F., Schurr, P. H. & Oh, S. (1987), 'Developing buyer–seller relationships', *Journal of Marketing*, 51, 11–27.

Freed, Richard, Freed, Shervin & Romano, Joe (1995), *Writing Winning Business Proposals*, McGraw Hill, New York.

Fuller, G. W. & Clydesdale, F. M. (1998), *Getting the Most Out of Your Consultant: A Guide to Selection through Implementation*, CRC Press, Boca Raton.

Ganesh, S. R. (1978), 'Organizational consultants: A comparison of styles', *Human Relations*, 31, 1–28.

Gill, J. & Whittle, S. (1992), 'Management by panacea', *Journal of Management Studies*, 30, 281–95.

Goffman, E. (1990), *The Presentation of Self in Everyday Life*, Penguin, Harmondsworth.

Harrison, Roger (1995), *Consultant's Journey: A Dance of Work and Spirit*, Jossey Bass, San Francisco.

—— (1995), *The Collected Papers of Roger Harrison*, Jossey Bass, San Francisco.

Hatcheul, Armand & Weil, Benoit (1995), *Experts in Organisations: A Knowledge Based Perspective on Organisational Change*, De Gruyter Studies in Organisation, Berlin.

Hill, C. W. L. & Pickering, J. F. (1986), 'Divisionalization, decentralization and performance of large UK companies', *Journal of Management Studies*, 23, 26–50.

Holmstrom, B. (1985), 'The provision of services in a market economy', in R. P. Inman (ed.), *Managing the Service Economy: Prospects and Problems*, Cambridge University Press, Cambridge.

Holz, Herman (1990), *Consultant's Guide to Writing Proposals*, John Wiley, New York.

—— (1998), *The Consultant's Guide to Getting Business on the Internet*, John Wiley, New York.

Kanter, R. M. (1989), 'The new managerial work', *Harvard Business Review*, November–December, 85–92.

Keeble, D., Bryson, J. & Wood, P. (1990), 'Small firms, business service growth and regional development in the UK: Some empirical findings', Small Business Research Centre working paper no. 7, University of Cambridge.

Kishel, Gregory F. & Kishel, Patricia (1996), *How to Start and Run a Successful Consulting Business*, John Wiley, New York.

Klein, B. & Leffler, K. B. (1981), 'The role of market forces in assuring contractual performance', *Journal of Political Economy*, 89, 615–41.

Levinson, Harry (1973), *The Great Jackass Fallacy*, Harvard University Press, Boston.

Lewin, Kurt (1951), *Field Theory in Social Science*, Harper, New York.

Lewin, Marsha D. (1995), *The Overnight Consultant*, John Wiley, New York.

Maister, David H. (1993), *Managing the Professional Service Firm*, The Free Press, New York.

Mangham, I. L. (1987), 'A matter of context', in I. L. Mangham (ed.), *Organization Analysis and Development*, Wiley, Chichester.

Mangham, I. L. & Overington, M. A. (1987), *Organizations as Theatre: A Social Psychology of Dramatic Appearances*, Wiley, Chichester.

Markham, Calvert (1993), *The Top Consultant: Developing Your Skills for Greater Effectiveness*, Kogan Page, London.

Peet, J. (1988), 'A survey of management consultancy: Outside looking in', *Economist*, 13 February, 1–19.

Pfarrer, Don (1998), *Guerrilla Persuasion: Mastering the Art of Effective and Winning Business Presentation*, Houghton Mifflin, Boston.

Popovich, Igor (1995), *Managing Consultants*, Random House, San Francisco.

Quay, John (1994), *Diagnostic Interviewing for Consultants and Auditors: A Collaborative Approach to Problem Solving*, 2nd edn, Quay Associates, Cincinatti.

Rathwell, J. M. (1974), *Marketing in the Service Sector*, Winthrop, Cambridge, Massachusetts.

Sashkin, M. & Burke, W. W. (1990), 'Organization development in the 1980s and an end-of-the-eighties retrospective', in F. Masarik (ed.), *Advances in Organization Development*, Ablex, Norwood, New Jersey.

Schaffer, Robert H. (1997), *High Impact Consulting: How Clients and Consultants can Leverage Rapid Results into Long Term Gains*, Jossey Bass/Simon & Schuster, San Francisco.

Scheidel, T. M. (1967), *Persuasive Speaking*, Scott, Foresman, Glennview, Illinois.

Schlegelmilch, B. B., Diamantopoulos, A. & Moore, S. A. (1992), 'The market for management consulting in Britain: An analysis of supply and demand', *Management Decisions*, 30, 46–54.

Shapiro, C. (1983), 'Premiums for high quality products as returns to reputations', *Quarterly Journal of Economics*, 43, 659–79.

Shenton, Howard (1990), *Shenton on Consulting: Success Strategies from the Consultant's Consultant*, John Wiley, New York.

Steele, Fritz (1982), *The Role of the Internal Consultant: Effective Role Shaping for Staff Positions*, CBI Publishing, Massachusetts.

Stock, J. R. & Zinszer, P. H. (1987), 'The industrial purchase decision for professional services', *Journal of Business Research*, 15, 1–16.

Tisdall, P. (1982), *Agents of Change: The Development and Practice of Management Consultancy*, Heinemann, London.

Walker, R. A. (1985), 'Is there a service economy? The changing capitalist division of labour', *Science and Society*, 49, 42–83.

Weisbord, Marvin (1992), *Discovering Common Ground*, Berrett Koehler, San Francisco.

Wilson, A. (1972), *The Marketing of Professional Services*, McGraw-Hill, London.

Woodworth, W. & Nelson, R. (1979), 'Witch doctors, messianics, sorcerers, and OD consultants: Parallels and paradigms', *Organizational Dynamics*, Autumn, 17–33.

World Bank (1998), *Selection of Consultants*, As outlined in the World
    Bank Guidelines—selection and employment of consultants by
    World Bank Borrowers, rev. edn, Washington.

JOURNAL OF MANAGEMENT CONSULTING† ARTICLES

1999 (vol. 10, no. 3)

The logic of management consulting
Not-for-profit consulting
Successful management consulting in Zimbabwe
Single white female
The art of writing an engagement letter
Think your way to clear writing
Developing strategy
Managing retention at Deloitte Consulting

1998 (vol. 10, nos 1 and 2)

Do proprietary tools lead to cookie cutter consulting
From executive to consultant and back again
Establishing referral sources
Forging stronger partnerships with your clients
Managing your argument
Keys to successful communication
Think your way to clear writing
An approach to organisational intervention
The logic of management consulting
Why and how Southwest Airlines uses management consultants
We created a monster
Compensation and benefits in consulting firms
High-technology and large-scale projects
How I got my ten largest assignments
Think your way to clear writing
How clients pick management consultants in Australia and New Zealand
Avoiding intervention pitfalls in international consulting

---

† In 2000, the journal changed its name to *Consulting to Management*.
    Web site: www.C2M.com

1997 (vol. 9, nos 3 and 4)

Ownership transfer
Planning for succession
Lessons from a buyout
On being acquired
Intellectual property in ownership transfers
Going public
Closing down your practice
Speak out, stand out
Developing new consulting products
Action in the boardroom
Looking in the mirror: Do we practice what we preach?
How to help computer projects succeed
Flowcharts: A powerful diagnostic tool
Two perspectives on consulting in Russia
Strategies for smaller firms
Consulting in a constellation of advice givers
Researching smaller companies

1996 (vol. 9, nos 1 and 2)

A consultant and *Gemba*
Involve the CEO
Two views of 'practice management'
Costs of doing business for solo practitioners and small firms
How to get and keep more business owners as clients
Appraising client needs
Consulting for fun and profit
A confederation of professionals
Training future consultants
Harnessing the power of electronic information
A lesson in how to attract new clients
Value-added fads
When clients resist change
A consultant's guide to Internet e-mail
The many ways to lure prospective clients
On filling the role of expert witness
The 13 cardinal sins
A historical view of the profession
Using ideas to increase the marketability of your firm

1995 (vol. 8, nos 3 and 4)

Consulting across East–West boundaries
The price of exceptional expertise
How UK consulting firms market
Strategic alliances
When clients make you crazy
Marketing consulting services on line
Consulting for results
Finessing the sale
Maximising consultancy income
The costs of doing business in 1994: A survey of expenses not re-billed to
    clients
How much bang for your buck: Measuring the value of marketing com-
    munications
Consulting to a joint venture: Satisfying the needs of multiple clients
    through competition
Sherlock Holmes on consulting
Five questions to resolve any conflict: An interactive article
Demand increases sharply for roaming managers

1994 (vol. 8, nos 1 and 2)

Consultancies need a brains approach
Getting consultants to sell
Team selling
Relocating a solo practice
Working together: Contractual relations for the management consultant
Agreements help make the practice
The consultant's role in re-engineering
Consultants: Is your firm ready for the next wave of office technology?
Transactions and games in consultant–client relations
How much money are you really making?
Personal goals: The base for goals as a consultant
So you want to go out on your own?
Strategic planning and the anatomy of change
Consulting to small business in Australia
Marketing consulting services using public relations strategies
Training the interviewee
Confidentiality and consultant agreements

1993 (vol. 7, no. 4)

Rethinking education
Implementing TQM on a shoestring
How to consult to government
A view from Quebec: Professional recognition as a social contribution
Engagement fees
A whole-brain approach to balance your life for management consultants
Management consulting in Greece: The profession is growing
Managing language can help consultants strengthen client relationships

1992 (vol. 7, no. 1)

The training and management of consultants
Daniel in the lion's den: Selling to groups
Excellence in presentation skills
Management consulting around the world
Managing the ongoing fee relationship
For professionals, the bottom line is not always the bottom line
Consultants as shamans
Rainmaking

References

Barcus, Sam W. 3rd & Wilkinson, Joseph W. (eds) (1995), *Handbook of Management Consulting Services*, 2nd edn, McGraw Hill, New York.

Bion, W. R. (1961), *Experiences in Groups*, Tavistock, London.

Block, P. (1981), *Flawless Consulting: A Guide to Getting Your Expertise Used*, Learning Concepts, Austin, Texas.

Clark, Timothy (1995), *Managing Consultants: Consultancy as the Management of Impressions*, Open University Press, Buckingham.

Coulson-Thomas, Colin (1997), 'The future of organisations', paper presented at the 5th Asia Pacific Conference of Management Consultants, Chennai, India, 8–9 December.

De Bono, Edward (1992), *Serious Creativity: Using the Power of Lateral Thinking to Create New Ideas*, Harper Business, New York.

Farson, Richard (1996), *Management of the Absurd*, Simon & Schuster, New York.

Gibson, Rowan (ed.) (1997), *Rethinking the Future*, Nicholas Brealey Publishing, Sonoma, California.

Goldratt, Eli (1990), *The Theory of Constraints and How it Should be Implemented*, North River Press, Croton-on-Hudson, New York.

Greenbaum, Thomas L. (1990), *The Consultant's Manual*, John Wiley & Sons, New York.

Greiner, L. E. & Metzger, R. O. (1983), *Consulting to Management*, Prentice Hall, Englewood Cliffs, New Jersey.

Harley, Bill (1998), 'The myth of empowerment: Work organisation, hierarchy and employee autonomy in contemporary Australian workplaces', Department of Management working paper in HRM and Industrial Relations, no. 4, March, University of Melbourne.

Harvey-Jones, John (1988), *Making It Happen: Reflections on Leadership*, William Collins & Sons, Glasgow.

Hutton, Geoffrey (1972a), 'Notes on research approaches and method', Bath University occasional paper, Centre for the Study of Organisational Change.

—— (1972b), *Thinking About Organisations*, 2nd edn, Tavistock, London.

171

—— (1979), 'Notes on research and consulting: Proverbs for practice', Bath University occasional paper, Centre for the Study of Organisational Change.

Ivancevich, John M., Lorenzi, Peter, Skinner, Steven J. & Crosby, Philip B. (1997), *Management: Quality and Competitiveness*, 2nd edn, Irwin, Chicago.

Janis, Irving L. (1972), *Victims of Groupthink: A Psychological Study of Foreign Policy Decisions and Fiascoes*, Houghton Mifflin, Boston.

Jaques, Elliott (1951), *The Changing Culture of a Factory*, Tavistock Publications Ltd, London.

Jaques, Elliott & Clement, Stephen D. (1991), *Executive Leadership: A Practical Guide to Managing Complexity*, Blackwell Business, Massachusetts.

Jarosch, Greg (1997), *Bench Marking Survey*, WA Chapter of IMC, Perth.

Katzenbach, Jon (1997), 'The myth of the top management team', *Harvard Business Review*, November–December, 83–91.

Keeble, D., Bryson, J. & Wood, P. (1994), *Pathfinders of Enterprise: The Creation, Growth and Dynamics of Small Management Consultancies in Britain*, Small Business Research Trust Business Services Research monograph no. 3, School of Management, The Open University, Milton Keynes.

Koestler, Arthur (1959), *The Sleepwalkers*, Grosset & Dunlap, New York.

Kubr, Milan (ed.) (1996), *Management Consulting: A Guide to the Profession*, 3rd (rev.) edn, International Labour Office, Geneva.

Machiavelli, Niccolo (1950), *The Prince, and the Discourses*, Modern Library, New York.

Mant, Alistair (1997), *Intelligent Leadership*, Allen & Unwin, St Leonards, New South Wales.

Micklethwait, John & Woolridge, Adrian (1996), *The Witch Doctors: Making Sense of the Management Gurus*, Times Books/Random House, New York.

Mintzberg, Henry (1973), *The Nature of Managerial Work*, Harper & Row, New York.

Napier, Rodney W. & Gershenfeld, Matti K. (1973), *Groups: Theory and Experience*, Houghton Mifflin Company, Boston.

Revans, R. W. (1982), *The Origins and Growth of Action Learning*, Chartwell-Bratt, Lund, Bromley.

Roszak, Theodore (1994), *The Cult of Information*, 2nd edn, University of California Press, Berkeley.

Schein, E. H. (1969), *Process Consultation: Its Role in Organisation Development*, Addison-Wesley, Reading.

Smith, Barry (1996), 'Where have the creators gone?, *HR Monthly*, March, 22.

Smith, Roger C. (1994), *Maxims for Managers*, Access Press, Perth.

Sofer, Cyril (1961), *The Organisation From Within*, Tavistock, London.

Steele, Fritz (1975), *Consulting for Organisational Change*, University of Massachusetts Press, Amherst.

Stoll, Clifford (1995), *Silicon Snake Oil: Second Thoughts on the Silicon Highway*, Doubleday, New York.

Weiss, Alan (1992), *Million Dollar Consulting: The Professional's Guide to Growing a Practice*, McGraw Hill, New York.

Winnicott, D. W. (1974), *Playing and Reality*, Penguin, Harmondsworth.

Younge, Gary (1999), 'Called to account', *Guardian* (UK), 30 August.